Grammar Dimensions
Book 2A

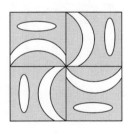

/

Grammar Dimensions

Book 2A
Form, Meaning, and Use

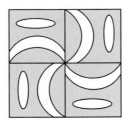

Heidi Riggenbach
University of Washington

Virginia Samuda
Sonoma State University

Heinle & Heinle Publishers
A Division of Wadsworth, Inc.
Boston, Massachusetts 02116 U.S.A

Photo Credits:

Photos on page 2 (photos 1–3) courtesy of H. Armstrong Roberts.

Photo on page 2 (photo 4) by J. Myers courtesy of H. Armstrong Roberts.

Photos on page 2 (photos 5, 6) courtesy of the University of Illinois.

Photo on page 2 (photo 7) courtesy of the *Illio,* University of Illinois yearbook.

Photo on page 38 of John Lennon courtesy of Kahana/Shooting Star.

Photo on page 177 of Diana Ross (recent) courtesy of Kahana/Shooting Star, page 178 (yearbook) courtesy of Seth Poppel Yearbook Archives.

Photo on page 177 of Tina Turner (recent) courtesy of McAfee/Shooting Star, page 178 (yearbook) courtesy of Seth Poppel Yearbook Archives.

Photo on page 177 of Madonna (recent) courtesy of Archer/Shooting Star, page 178 (yearbook) courtesy of Seth Poppel Yearbook Archives.

Photo on page 177 of Meryl Streep (recent) courtesy of Leonelli/Shooting Star, page 178 (yearbook) courtesy of Seth Poppel Yearbook Archives.

Photo on page 177 of Bruce Springsteen (recent) courtesy of Gallo/Shooting Star, page 178 (yearbook) courtesy of Seth Poppel Yearbook Archives.

Photo on page 177 of Warren Beatty (recent) courtesy of Fotex/Shooting Star, page 178 (yearbook) courtesy of Seth Poppel Yearbook Archives.

The publication of the Grammar Dimensions series
was directed by the members of the Heinle & Heinle
ESL Publishing Team:

David C. Lee, Editorial Director
Susan Mraz, Marketing Manager
Lisa McLaughlin, Production Editor
Nancy Mann, Developmental Editor

Also participating in the publication of this program were:

Publisher: Stanley J. Galek
Editorial Production Manager: Elizabeth Holthaus
Assistant Editor: Kenneth Mattsson
Manufacturing Coordinator: Mary Beth Lynch
Full Service Production/Design: Publication Services, Inc.
Cover Designer: Martucci Studio
Cover Artist: Susan Johnson

10 9 8 7 6 5 4 3 2 1

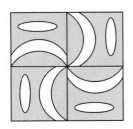

Book 2A Table of Contents
(see page X for Book 2B Table of Contents)

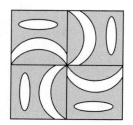

Book 2B Table of Contents

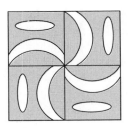

Preface to *Grammar Dimensions: Form, Meaning, and Use*

To the Teacher

ABOUT THE SERIES

With the recent emphasis on communication, the teaching of grammar has often been downplayed, or even overlooked entirely. Although one would not want to argue the goal of having students be able to communicate successfully, it is important to recognize that a major means to this end is to teach students to use grammatical structures. Some grammatical structures may be acquired naturally without instruction, but it is assumed by the creators of this series that explicit focus on the troublesome aspects of English will facilitate and accelerate their acquisition. The teaching needs to be done, however, in such a way that the interdependence of grammar and communication is appreciated.

In this regard, it is crucial to recognize that the use of grammatical structures involves more than having students achieve formal accuracy. Students must be able to use the structures meaningfully and appropriately as well. This series, therefore, takes into account all three dimensions of language: syntax/morphology (form), semantics (meaning), and pragmatics (use). The relevant facts about the **form, meaning,** and **use** of English grammatical structures were compiled into a comprehensive scope and sequence and distributed across a four-book series. Where the grammatical system is complex (e.g., the verb-tense system) or the structure complicated (e.g., the passive voice), it is revisited in each book in the series. Nevertheless, each book is free-standing and may be used independently of the others in the series if the student or program needs warrant.

Another way in which the interdependence of grammar and communication is stressed is that students first encounter every structure in a meaningful context where their attention is not immediately drawn to its formal properties. Each treatment of a grammatical structure concludes with students being given the opportunity to use the structure in communicative activities. The point of the series is not to teach grammar as static knowledge, but to have students use it in the dynamic process of communication. In this way grammar might better be thought of as a skill, rather than as an area of knowledge.

It is my hope that this book will provide teachers with the means to create, along with their students, learning opportunities that are tailored to learners' needs, are enjoyable, and will maximize everyone's learning.

ABOUT THE BOOK

This book deals with basic sentence and subsentence grammatical structures. It also introduces language forms that support certain social functions such as making requests and seeking permission.

Units that share certain features have been clustered together. No more than three or four units are clustered at one time, however, in order to provide for some variety of focus. As the units have been designed to stand independently, it is possible for a syllabus to be constructed that follows a different order of structures than the one presented in the book. It is also not expected that there will be sufficient time to deal with all the material that has been introduced here within a single course. Teachers are encouraged to see the book as a resource from which they can select units or parts of units which best meet student needs.

Unit Organization

TASKS

One way in which to identify student needs is to use the **Tasks**, which open each unit as a pre-test. Learner engagement in the Tasks may show that students have already learned what they need to know about a certain structure, in which case the unit can be skipped entirely. Or it may be possible, from examining students' performance, to pinpoint precisely where the students need to work. For any given structure, the learning challenge presented by the three dimensions of language is not equal. Some structures present more of a form-based challenge to learners; for others, the long-term challenge is to learn what the structures mean or when to use them. The type and degree of challenge varies according to the inherent complexity of the structure itself and the particular language background and level of English proficiency of the students.

FOCUS BOXES

Relevant facts about the form, meaning, and use of the structure are presented in **Focus Boxes** following the Task. Teachers can work their way systematically through a given unit or can pick and choose from among the Focus Boxes those points on which they feel students specifically need to concentrate.

EXERCISES

From a pedagogical perspective, it is helpful to think of grammar as a skill to be developed. Thus, in this book, **Exercises** have been provided to accompany each Focus Box. Certain of the Exercises may be done individually, others with students working in pairs or in small groups. Some of the Exercises can be done in class, others assigned as homework. Students' learning styles and the learning challenge they are working on will help teachers determine the most effective way to have students use the Exercises. (The Instructor's Manual should be consulted also for helpful hints in this regard.)

ACTIVITIES

At the end of each unit are a series of **Activities** that help students realize the communicative value of the grammar they are learning and that offer them further practice in using the grammar to convey meaning. Teachers or students may select the Activities from which they believe they would derive the most benefit and enjoyment. Student performance on these Activities can be used as a post-test as well. Teachers should not expect perfect performance at this point, however. Often there is a delayed effect in learning anything, and even some temporary backsliding in student performance as new material is introduced.

OTHER COMPONENTS

An **Instructor's Manual** is available for this book. The Manual contains answers to the Exercise questions and grammatical notes where pertinent. The Manual also further discusses the theory underlying the series and "walks a teacher through" a typical unit, suggesting ways in which the various components of the unit might be used and supplemented in the classroom.

A student **Workbook** also accompanies this book. It provides additional exercises to support the material presented in this text. Many of the workbook exercises are specially designed to help students prepare for the TOEFL (Test of English as a Foreign Language).

Each level of Grammar Dimensions is available in split editions (A and B) or as a complete text. The split editions are ideal for short course or classes which move at a gradual pace.

To the Student

All grammar structures have a form, a meaning, and a use. We can show this with a pie chart:

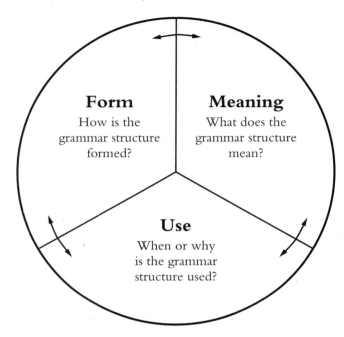

Often you will find that you know the answer to one or more of these questions, but not to all of them, for a particular grammar structure. This book has been written to help you learn answers to these questions for the major grammar structures of English. More importantly, it gives you practice with the answers so that you can develop your ability to use English grammar structures accurately, meaningfully, and appropriately.

At the beginning of each unit, you will be asked to work on a **Task.** The Task will introduce you to the grammar structures to be studied in the unit. However, it is not important at this point that you think about grammar. You should just do the Task as well as you can.

In the next section of the unit are **Focus Boxes** and **Exercises.** You will see that the boxes are labeled with **FORM, MEANING, USE,** or a combination of these, corresponding to the three parts of the pie chart. In each Focus Box is information that answers one or more of the questions in the pie. Along with the Focus Box are Exercises that should help you put into practice what you have studied.

The last section of each unit contains communicative **Activities.** Hopefully, you will enjoy doing these and at the same time receive further practice using the grammar structures in meaningful ways.

By working on the Task, studying the Focus Boxes, doing the Exercises, and engaging in the Activities, you will develop greater knowledge of English grammar and skill in using it. I also believe you will enjoy the learning experience along the way.

Diane Larsen-Freeman

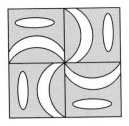

Acknowledgments

Series Director Acknowledgments

As with any project this ambitious, a number of people have made important contributions. I need to thank my students in the MAT Program at the School for International Training and audiences worldwide for listening to me talk about my ideas for reconciling the teaching of grammar with communicative language teaching. Their feedback and questions have been invaluable in the evolution of my thinking. One student, Anna Mussman, should be singled out for her helpful comments on the manuscript that she was able to provide based on her years of English teaching. A number of other anonymous teacher reviewers have also had a formative role in the development of the series. I hope they derive some satisfaction in seeing that their concerns were addressed wherever possible. In addition, Marianne Celce-Murcia not only helped with the original scope and sequence of the series, but also provided valuable guidance throughout its evolution.

I feel extremely grateful, as well, for the professionalism of the authors, who had to put into practice the ideas behind this series. Their commitment to the project, patience with its organic nature, and willingness to keep at it are all much appreciated. I insisted that the authors be practicing ESL teachers. I believe the series has benefited from this decision, but I am also cognizant of the demands it has put on the authors' lives these past few years.

Finally, I must acknowledge the support of the Heinle and Heinle "team." This project was "inherited" by Heinle and Heinle during its formative stage. To Dave Lee, Susan Mraz, Lisa McLaughlin, and especially Susan Maguire, who never stopped believing in this project, I am indeed thankful. And to Nancy Mann, who helped the belief become a reality, I am very grateful.

Author Acknowledgments

We would like to thank our families, friends, students, colleagues, cats—and each other—for hanging in there. We would also like to thank Diane Larsen-Freeman for her guidance during the process of writing this book, and the following reviewers for their valuable suggestions: Brian Hickey (Manhattanville College), Marilyn Santos (Valencia Community College), Marjore Walsleben (UCLA), Martha Low (University of Oregon), Jonathan Seeley (University of Arizona), and the field tester, Mary Monogue (University of Colorado, Boulder).

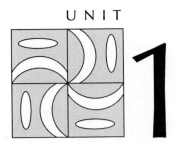

Simple Present
Facts, Habits, and Routines

Task

How Do You Learn Grammar?

Complete this questionnaire about the way you learn by circling the number beside each statement.

1 = never true for me	2 = rarely true for me	3 = sometimes true for me	4 = often true for me	5 = always true for me

1. I take every opportunity to practice the the English I know.   1 2 3 4 5
2. To learn grammar, I study grammar books and memorize the rules.   1 2 3 4 5
3. To learn grammar, I read newspapers, watch TV and movies, and listen to songs.   1 2 3 4 5
4. When I don't know how to say something exactly, I don't say anything at all.   1 2 3 4 5
5. To learn grammar, I observe native speakers in different situations and notice what they say and do.   1 2 3 4 5
6. I am not afraid of making mistakes because mistakes help me learn.   1 2 3 4 5
7. Working in groups with my classmates helps me learn.   1 2 3 4 5
8. I ask questions when I do not understand.   1 2 3 4 5
9. When I can't think of how to say something, I try to say it another way.   1 2 3 4 5
10. I try to think in English.   1 2 3 4 5
11. I think of grammar rules when I speak.   1 2 3 4 5

Now compare your answers with those of another student. In what ways are your learning habits similar and in what ways are they different? What other things do you do to learn grammar? Share and compare your findings with the rest of the class and with your teacher.

Focus 1

Simple Present Tense

USE

- The simple present talks about habits: things you do again and again.
    (a) I ask questions when I don't understand.
- The simple present also talks about everyday routines: things you do regularly.
    (b) My sister gets up at 6:00.

Focus 2

FORM

Simple Present Tense

Statement	Negative	Question	Short Answers
I You We They } work.	I You We They } do not/don't work.	Do { I you we they } work?	Yes, { I you we they } do.
He She It } works.	He She It } does not/doesn't work.	Does { he she it } work?	Yes, { he she it } does.
			No, { I you we they } don't.
			No, { he she it } doesn't.

Exercise 1

What are some of the *other* things you do (or do not do) to help you learn English grammar? Complete the following, using full sentences.

Some things I do:

1. I _____ .

2. I _____ .

3. I _____ .

Some things I don't do:

1. I _____ .

2. I _____ .

3. I _____ .

Now share your sentences with a partner. Then, without showing your books to each other, write about your partner here.

My partner, _____ (name), does several different things to learn English.

She or he _____ .

_____ .

_____ .

Now get together with a *different* partner. Tell him or her what you and your first partner do (and do not do) to learn English grammar. Compare your findings with your new partner's findings. Together with your new partner, decide on the three most useful strategies that you and your partners use. Share your findings with the rest of the class.

Focus 3

FORM ● MEANING

Adverbs of Frequency

FORM
MEANING

- To show **how often** you do something, you can use an adverb of frequency:

**Most
Frequently**

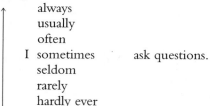

always
usually
often
I   sometimes   ask questions.
seldom
rarely
hardly ever
never

**Least
Frequently**

Position of Adverbs of Frequency	
Before the main verb: **(a)** I **usually** get up at 6:00. **(b)** He **never** calls me.	After the verb *be:* **(c)** She is **always** late. **(d)** They are **rarely** happy.

- For more information on adverbs of frequency, see Unit 16, Focus 7.

Exercise 2

Complete the chart with information about the habits and routines of these people when they are in the classroom. The first one has been done for you as an example.

	Teachers in My Country	Students in My Country	Teachers in This Country	Students in This Country
Usually	give a lot of homework			
Sometimes				
Hardly ever				
Never				

Now get together with a student from another country, if possible, and ask eight questions about the information from his or her chart:

What do { teachers / students } in your country { usually / sometimes / hardly ever / never } do?

Now make as many true sentences as you can, using the information from your chart (and from your partner's if possible).

EXAMPLE: *Students in this country never stand up when the teacher enters the classroom.*

Exercise 3

Read the job descriptions below and match them to the occupations in the list below.

1. He wears a uniform and usually travels many miles a day. He serves food and drink, but he hardly ever prepares them himself.

2. She works in an office, but she often takes work home with her. She generally earns a high salary, but often feels a lot of stress. She sometimes entertains clients in the evening.

3. He usually wears a uniform and always carries a gun. He leads a dangerous life, so his job rarely gets boring.

4. He often works at night and meets many different people. He serves drinks and gets tips when people like his work.

5. She wears a uniform and drives many miles a day. She never serves food or drinks.

6. He spends many hours in the classroom and asks questions. He always has a lot of work to do and sometimes writes on the blackboard.

7. She often wears a uniform and walks many miles a day. She works very hard and does not earn very much money, although she sometimes gets generous tips.

8. They spend a lot of time in the classroom and like to ask questions. They often write on the blackboard.

a student	a policeman	a businesswoman	secretaries
	a flight attendant	mechanics	teachers
a nurse	a bartender	an architect	a bus driver	a waitress

Now write similar descriptions for the jobs that are still left in the box.

9. _____

_____

10. _____

_____

11. _____

_____

12. _____

_____

Now think of two more jobs. Write a short job description for each one and get together with another student. Read your descriptions to each other and ask and answer questions until you guess the jobs your partner has described:

EXAMPLE: Does she or he . . . ?

Is she or he a . . . ?

13. _____

_____

14. _____

_____

Exercise 4

Sam is looking for a roommate to share his house, and Dave is looking for a place to live. They are trying to find out if they will be compatible as roommates. Complete their conversation, using verbs that will complete the meaning. Sometimes more than one answer is possible.

Sam: What do you usually do on weekends?

Dave: Well, I usually (1) _____ early, about 5:30, and then I (2) _____

by the river for an hour or so before breakfast.

Sam: Really? And what (3) _____ you _____ next?

Dave: After breakfast, I (4) _____ a cold shower, and then I usually

(5) _____ my bike or I sometimes (6) _____ tennis for a couple

of hours. What (7) _____ you _____ on Saturday mornings?

Sam: I like to relax on weekends; I (8) _____ home and (9) _____

the newspaper and (10) _____ TV.

Dave: All weekend?

Sam: No. On Sundays, I often get in my sports car and (11) _____ to the beach.

Dave: Great! I like swimming too. My brother (12) _____ in the ocean every day

of the year, even in the winter.

Sam: Well, I rarely (13) _____ in the ocean. I usually (14) _____ on

the beach and try to get a good sun tan. Then I (15) _____ some of my

friends and we go to a bar and (16) _____ beer.

Dave: Don't you ever exercise?

Sam: Well, I (17) _____ (not) to a health club or gym, but every Saturday night, I

go to a disco and I (18) _____ for hours. That's my idea of exercise.

7

Focus 4

Simple Present Tense

USE

- You can also use simple present to talk about statements of **fact**—things that are always true:

    The sun **rises** in the east and sets in the west.

- Thus, we use the simple present to talk about routines, habits, and facts.

Exercise 5

Match these facts by connecting the information in Column A with the appropriate information in Column B.

A   **B**

Horses   have twelve eyes.

Scorpions   live for about two years.

Spiders   sleep standing up.

Elephants   use their ears to "see."

Ducks   run at a speed of 70 miles per hour.

Antelopes   stay with the same mate all their lives.

Bats   sometimes go for four days without water.

Do you know any other unusual facts about animals or insects? Share them with the rest of the class.

Activities

Activity 1

The purpose of this activity is to *prove* or *disprove* the following statements about your classmates. Survey your classmates by asking questions to see if the following are true or false.

1. Most people in this class do not eat breakfast.

2. Women drink more coffee than men.

3. Three people come to school by bike.

4. The people in this room sleep an average of seven hours a night.

5. 50 percent of the people here watch TV every night.

6. At least half of the people in this room smoke.

7. At least three people wear contact lenses.

8. The people in this room have an average of three brothers and sisters.

9. Most people in this room do not like opera.

10. At least half of the people here read a newspaper in English every day.

Activity 2

The purpose of this activity is to find out what North Americans usually do on certain special days. Interview several different people (native speakers if possible) and find out what usually happens on these days. Share your findings with the class.

St. Patrick's Day:_____

_____

Valentine's Day:_____

_____

Thanksgiving Day:_____

_____

Halloween:_____

_____

Activity 3

Complete the following with information that is true about yourself. Write complete sentences.

SOMETHING I USUALLY DO IN SUMMER:_____

_____

SOMETHING I OFTEN DO ON WEEKENDS:_____

_____

SOMETHING I RARELY DO IN THIS COUNTRY:_____

_____

SOMETHING I SOMETIMES DO ON FRIDAYS:_____

_____

1. Memorize these four sentences about yourself.
2. Walk around the room. When your teacher tells you to stop, find the nearest person. Tell her or him your four sentences. When she or he tells you *her or his* sentences, memorize them.
3. Walk around the room. When your teacher tells you to stop, find a different person. Tell him or her about the habits of **the last person you spoke to**. Do not talk about your own. Memorize what he or she tells you.
4. Find someone different. Tell him or her **the information the last person told you**. Memorize what he or she tells you.
5. Now find someone new. Continue the process for as long as possible. Remember, you always pass along **the information the last person tells you**. Try to speak to as many different people as possible.
6. At the end, tell the rest of the class the information you heard from the last person. Is all the information true?

Activity 4

Write a letter to a friend or family member describing what usually happens in your English classes or what you usually do on weekends here.

Activity 5

Prepare a short talk for your classmates, describing a special day or holiday that people celebrate in your country, city, or region. Talk about what people usually do on this day and how they celebrate.

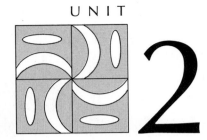

2

Present Progressive
Stative and Nonstative Verbs

Task

What do you think is probably happening in this picture? Draw the missing parts and be ready to describe your interpretation of the picture to the rest of the class. Decide who has the most interesting theory.

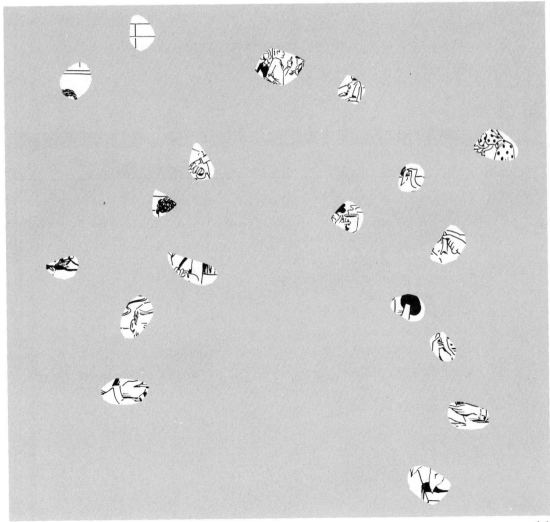

Focus 1

Present Progressive

USE

- Use verbs in the present progressive to talk about actions and situations that are **in progress** or in the middle of happening at the time of speaking:

    (a) Right now, I **am sitting** on the couch and my brothers **are cooking** dinner.

    (b) It **is raining** at the moment and Oscar **is waiting** for the bus.

- You may also use the present progressive to talk about actions and situations that are going on **around** the time of speaking, although they may not be in progress **exactly** at the time of speaking. These actions or situations are often temporary, and we expect them to end in the future:

    (c) This semester, I **am taking** three math classes.

- Some common time expressions associated with present progressive:

    right now   this year
    at the moment   this semester
    today   this week
    at present   these days

Exercise 1

Look at the following statements about the picture in the Task and decide which ones are *probably* true (T) and which ones are *probably* false (F).

1. Some coats are hanging on a rack.   T   F
2. A customer in a restaurant is checking the bill.   T   F
3. Somebody is typing.   T   F
4. Somebody is gardening.   T   F
5. Somebody is writing a letter.   T   F
6. Several people are waiting to see a doctor in a hospital. T   F

Now look at the complete picture on page 22. How many of your guesses were correct?

Focus 2

Present Progressive

- To form the present progressive, use *be* + *present participle* (*-ing*) of the main verb:

Statement	Negative	Question	Short Answers
I am (I'm) working.	I am not (I'm not) working.	Am I working?	Yes, I am. No, I'm not.
You are (you're) work-ing.	You are not (aren't) working.	Are you working?	Yes, you are. No, you aren't. OR You're not.
She/He/It is (She's/He's/It's) working.	She/He/It is not (isn't) working.	Is she/he/it working?	Yes, she/he/it is. No, she/he/it isn't. OR She's/He's/It's not.
We are (We're) work-ing.	We are not (aren't) working.	Are we working?	Yes, we are. No we aren't. OR we're not.
They are (They're) working.	They are not (aren't) working.	Are they working?	Yes, they are. No, they aren't OR They're not.

Exercise 2

Study the complete picture in the Task for one minute. Turn the page and, from memory, write as many sentences as possible to describe what is going on in the picture. Compare your results with those of the rest of the class. Who can remember the most?

Focus 3

Simple Present versus
Present Progressive

USE

- Use the simple present tense to talk about events or actions that happen regularly and repeatedly (see Unit 1). Thus, the simple present refers to permanent or habitual situations.

  (a) Philippe **smokes** 20 cigarettes a day.

- Use the present progressive to talk about events or actions that are already going on **at** the time of speaking or **around** the time of speaking. Thus, the present progressive refers to temporary situations:

  (b) Philippe **is smoking** a cigarette right now.

  (c) Philippe **is smoking** more cigarettes than usual these days because he is nervous about his final exams.

Exercise 3

Complete the following using either simple present or present progressive. Use the words in parentheses. The first one has been done for you.

1. A: Ray! The phone *is ringing* (ring).

    B: I can't get it. I _____ (wash) my hair.

2. A: Look at Juan. He _____ (smoke).

    B: That's strange. He _____ (smoke + never)!

    A: Maybe he's nervous about something.

3. A: Hey, Pam! What a surprise! What _____ you _____

    (do) on campus?

    B: I _____ (take) an art class this semester. It's great!

    I _____ (learn) a lot.

4. A: Please be quiet, we _____ (study) for a test!

    B: What kind of test?

    A: Math. We _____ (have + always) a math test on Mondays.

5. (The phone rings.)

   A: Hi, honey. How_____ you _____ (do)?

   B: Mom! What a coincidence! I was about to write you a letter.

   A: Really? You _____ (write + hardly ever) me letters. Is some-

   thing wrong?

6. A: What's the matter?

   B: It _____ (rain) and I _____

   (have + not) an umbrella.

7. A: Why _____ Brian _____ (wear) a

   suit today?

   B: It's Tuesday. He _____ (go + always) to lunch with his boss

   on Tuesdays.

8. A: I have to find a different roommate.

   B: Why?

   A: Because my current roommate and I have completely different life-styles. For example, she

   _____ (get up) early, but I _____

   (sleep) late. We _____ (like + not) the same food; she

   _____ (eat + not) meat or fish or eggs. It's really hard sharing

   an apartment.

   A: Why don't you two get together right now and talk the problem over? What

   _____ she _____ (do) at the moment?

   B: She _____ (sleep). She _____ (go

   + always) to bed at 8:00.

Exercise 4

Can you translate the following into English? Write your answers below. After that, underline the verbs in each sentence and write each verb in the appropriate box. The first one has been done for you.

1. 👁 ♡ U. *I love you*

2. 👁 C U. _____

3. 👁 H ÷ 8 U. _____

4. 👁 H ÷ 🙂 U. _____

5. He 👎 U. _____

6. R U 21 ? _____

7. 👁 C U R YY 4 me. _____

8. 👁 TH ÷ 🕯 UR GR ÷ 8. _____

You can find the answers to this puzzle on page 22.

Now underline all the verbs in your sentences and write them in the appropriate boxes below. The first one has been done for you.

```
┌─────────────────────────────┐      ┌─────────────────────────────┐
│     Verbs that express      │      │     Verbs that express      │
│    emotions and feelings    │      │    senses and perceptions   │
│                             │      │                             │
│            love             │      │                             │
│                             │      │                             │
│                             │      │                             │
└─────────────────────────────┘      └─────────────────────────────┘

┌─────────────────────────────┐
│     Verbs that express      │
│   cognition: knowledge,     │
│    thoughts, and beliefs    │
│                             │
│                             │
│                             │
└─────────────────────────────┘
```

Which verb does not fit into these boxes? _____
All these verbs have something in common. Can you tell what it is?

Focus 4

Stative Verbs

MEANING

- Some verbs are not used in the progressive in English. These are called **stative** because they refer to states which we do not expect to change, not actions which may be temporary.

    (a) He **loves** me, but he **hates** my cats.
    NOT: He **is loving** me, but he **is hating** my cats.

    (b) I **know** your sister.
    NOT: I **am knowing** your sister.

- The most common stative verbs are in these categories:

Emotion		Perception	Cognition	Possession
love	*prefer*	*see*	*think*	*have*
like	*want*	*hear*	*believe*	*own*
hate	*dislike*	*taste*	*know*	*belong*
appreciate		*smell*	*understand*	

Other Common Stative Verbs		
be	*need*	*owe*
seem	*weigh*	*cost*
exist		

Exercise 5

Complete the following with simple present or present progressive, using the verbs in parentheses.

Today, more and more people (1) _____ (discover) the joys of riding a bicycle.

In fact, mountain biking (2) _____ (become) one of America's most popu-

lar recreational activities. The bicycle business (3) _____ (grow) fast, and every

year it (4) _____ (produce) hundreds of new-model bikes. In general, bike shops

(5) _____ (sell) not only bicycles but also a full range of accessories and equipment.

Paul Brownstein (6) _____ (manage) a popular bike shop in Boston. Many of his customers (7) _____ (be) avid cyclists, and several (8) _____ (own) more than one bicycle. These people usually (9) _____ (ride) several times a week for pleasure, although according to Paul, more and more people these days (10) _____ (ride) their bicycles to work too, because they (11) _____ (believe) that bicycles (12) _____ (provide) an alternative to the automobile. Paul(13) _____ (sell) all kinds of bikes, but these days he (14) _____ (sell) a lot of bicycle clothing as well. In fact, one of his customers regularly (15) _____ (come) into the shop and (16) _____ (buy) clothes, even though she (17) _____ (not + own) a bicycle. She (18) _____ (like) the clothes, but (19) _____ (hate) the sport! Unfortunately, this attitude (20) _____ (not + be) unusual these days, because as everybody (21) _____ (know), some people (22) _____ (think) style and appearance (23) _____ (be) more important than anything else in life.

Focus 5

MEANING

Stative versus Nonstative Meaning

MEANING

- Stative verbs usually express a regular state or quality, **not** an action:
  (a) I love you.
  (b) I hate my job.
- Some verbs look like stative verbs because they describe a state, but they also have nonstative meanings when they describe action:

State	Action
(c) I weigh 120 pounds.	I am weighing myself (to see if I have gained weight).
(d) Mmm—dinner smells great!	I'm smelling the milk (to see if it is spoiled).
(e) The soup tastes good.	He is tasting the soup (to see if it needs salt).

- Therefore, when these verbs express a nonstative meaning, they can take the progressive forms.
  - *Be* is generally considered a stative verb because it describes a regular state or quality:
    (f) She is very polite.
  - *Have* is considered a stative verb when it describes possession:
    (g) She has a dog and two cats.
- However, when you use *have* to describe an experience and not possession, you use the progressive forms:

Possession	Experience
(h) They have three cars.	**(i)** We are having fun.

- Some common expressions using *have* and expressing an experience:

  have fun   *have a good time*   *have trouble with*
  have problems   *have difficulty with*

- When *have* describes a medical condition or physical discomfort, it does not usually take progressive forms:
    (j) I can't talk to you right now because I **have** a really sore throat.
    (k) Sandy **has** a headache and a high fever today; maybe she **has** the flu.

Exercise 6

Work with a partner or in a small group. You need a die and a small object (like a coin) to represent each person. First, take turns throwing the die. The person who throws the highest number starts. Put your coins (or objects) on the square marked *Start* on the following page. Throw the die and move your coin to the appropriate square. Complete the sentence in the square; if everyone agrees with your answer, you may write it in the square. If you are not sure, your teacher will be the referee. If you make a mistake or do not know the answer, you miss your next turn. The winner is the first person to reach the final square.

I _____ (love) grammar! 25	A: The chef _____ (taste) the food right now. B: Is it good? A: Yes! It _____ (taste) wonderful! 26	MISS A TURN 27	Did you cut your hand? It _____ (bleed). 28
She _____ (write) a letter now, but she rarely _____ (write) letters. 24	MISS A TURN 23	The students _____ (have) some trouble with verbs today. 22	She _____ (take) three classes this semester, but she usually _____ (take) more. 21
MISS A TURN 17	How many pairs of shoes _____ she _____ (own) now? 18	This suitcase _____ (weigh) too much. I can't carry it. 19	A: What's wrong? B: I _____ (have) problems with my boyfriend at the moment. 20
A: Look! There's the President B: Where? I _____ (not + see) him. 16	A: _____ you _____ (like) your job? B: No, I _____ (hate) it. 15	A: _____ you always _____ (take) the bus? B: No, I usually _____ (walk) to work. 14	A: Where's Tim? B: I _____ (think) he _____ (take) a nap. 13
A: How are the kids? B: They both _____ (have) sore throats today. 9	A: Shhh! We _____ (study) for a test. 10	A: _____ you _____ (like) Mexican food? B: Yes, I _____ (love) it! 11	A: How's Joe? B: Great. He _____ (have) fun because he _____ (have) a new car. 12
MISS A TURN 8	Mmm! Is that a new perfume? You _____ (smell) great. 7	What _____ you _____ (think) Henry _____ (think) about right now? 6	People _____ (spend) less money on entertainment these days. 5
START 1	Moya always _____ (sit) at the back of the class, but today she _____ (sit) at the front. 2	Rose _____ (not + know) that it is my birthday today. 3	MISS A TURN 4

Activities

Activity 1

Go to a crowded place where you can safely sit and watch what is happening around you. Look carefully at everything that is happening. Pretend you are a journalist or radio or television reporter. Describe in writing everything that you see. Do not forget to include everything you hear as well.

Activity 2

Work with a partner or a small group and develop a short story including a sequence of actions and emotions. Act out your story without using words. Your classmates must try to guess what is happening in your story by providing a commentary of everything your group does, as they watch it happen.

Activity 3

Do you know how to play tic-tac-toe? In this activity, you will be playing a version of this well-known game. Work with a partner or in teams. First copy each of the following onto separate cards or different pieces of paper. Place these cards facedown on the table in front of you.

she/speak	they/think about	he/believe
we/hear	she/dance (?)★	you/write (?)★
I/understand	we/sing	you/live
they/eat	they/work(?)★	I/see

(?)★ = make a question

The first player chooses a tic-tac-toe square and draws the first card. She or he makes a meaningful statement including the words in the tic-tac-toe square and the words on the card. Each statement must have *at least* four words in it (not including the words in the tic-tac-toe square). If everyone accepts your statement, you may mark the square with either *X* or *O*. The next player chooses a different square and draws the next card. The first person to draw a straight line through three squares is the winner. You may play this game repeatedly by erasing the *Xs* and *Os* at the end of each round, or by writing them on small pieces of paper and covering the squares with these. Good luck!

every day	*today*	*usually*
this week	*occasionally*	*right now*
often	*at the moment*	*sometimes*

ANSWERS TO EXERCISE 4

1. I love you.
3. I hate you.
5. He knows you.
7. I see you are too wise for me!

2. I see you.
4. I hear you.
6. Are you 21?
8. I think you are great.

Be Going To and Will

Task

In North America, Chinese restaurants traditionally give customers a fortune cookie at the end of the meal. This cookie is small and hollow. Inside you find a piece of paper that predicts something about your future. Can you match the two parts of these fortunes?

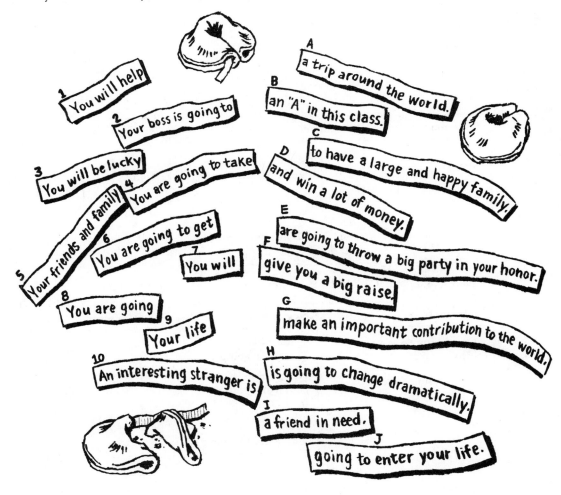

1. You will help
2. Your boss is going to
3. You will be lucky
4. You are going to take
5. Your friends and family
6. You are going to get
7. You will
8. You are going
9. Your life
10. An interesting stranger is

A. a trip around the world.
B. an "A" in this class.
C. to have a large and happy family.
D. and win a lot of money.
E. are going to throw a big party in your honor.
F. give you a big raise.
G. make an important contribution to the world.
H. is going to change dramatically.
I. a friend in need.
J. going to enter your life.

Focus 1

Talking about the Future with *Will* and *Be Going To*

MEANING

- To talk about the future, you can use *be going to* and *will*:
  - **(a)** It **will** rain some time next week.
  - **(b)** It **is going to** rain in a few minutes.

Focus 2

FORM

Will and *Be Going To*

FORM

- *Will* is a modal auxiliary and does not change form to agree with the subject:

Statement	Negative	Question
I You We They } **will** leave. **'ll**	I You We They } **will not/won't** leave.	**Will** { I you we they } leave?
He She It } **will** leave. **'ll**	He She It } **will not/won't** leave.	**Will** { he she it } leave?

- *Be going to* is a phrasal modal and changes form to agree with the subject:

Statement	Negative	Question
I { **am going to** leave. **'m**	I { **am not** **'m not going to** leave.	**Am** I **going to** leave?
He She It } **is going to** leave. **'s**	He She It } **is not** **isn't going to** leave. **'s not**	**Is** { he she it } **going to** leave?
You We They } **are going to** leave. **'re**	You We They } **are not** **aren't going to** leave. **'re not**	**Are** { I you we they } **going to** leave?

Exercise 1

Write the complete predictions about the future from the fortune cookies in the Task.

1. _____ .

2. _____ .

3. _____ .

4. _____ .

5. _____ .

6. _____ .

7. _____ .

8. _____ .

9. _____ .

10. _____ .

Focus 3

USE

Be Going To versus Will: Immediacy and Formality

USE

- Both *be going to* and *will* are used to make predictions. However, you use *be going to* for actions or events that you believe will occur very soon:

  (a) We're going to leave. (very soon)

  (b) We'll leave some time next week.

- *Will* is more formal than *be going to*; therefore, the choice of *be going to* over *will* also depends on the situation and the relationship between the speakers:

  (c) Mother to child: Daddy is going to be angry about this.

  (d) School principal to student: Your father will be angry about this.

Exercise 2

For each of the following, decide on the best form to use: *be going to* or *will*. In some sentences, it is possible to use both. The first one has been done for you.

1. Quick! Catch the baby! I think he _is going to_ fall off the sofa.

2. Excuse me, Mr. President. Do you think unemployment _____ decrease in the foreseeable future?

3. Uh-oh. Look at those clouds. It _____ rain.

4. I predict that you _____ meet a tall, dark, and handsome stranger and you _____ fall in love and get married.

5. One day we _____ look back at all this and laugh.

6. I don't believe it. Look at Paula! I think she _____ ask that guy to dance with her.

7. A: What do you think about my son's chances of getting into Harvard, Dr. Heath?

   B: I don't think he _____ have any problems at all, Mrs. Lee.

8. Meteorologists predict that the drought _____ end sometime this fall.

Focus 4

USE

Be Going To versus *Will:*
Plans and Intentions

USE

- *Be going to* also talks about future plans and intentions:
  (a) We are going to spend the month of August in Italy. We bought the tickets last week, and we are going to leave on August 3.
- *Be going to* is preferred to *will* here because it refers to plans that have already been made.

Exercise 3

In this exercise, you need to get information from one of your classmates. Use *be going to* or *will* in your answers, as appropriate.

1. Get together with a partner and find out three things she or he intends to do after class:

   My partner_____

   _____ .

2. Now find out three things she or he does not intend to do after class:

   My partner_____

   _____ .

3. Now make three predictions about your partner's future:

   My partner_____

   _____ .

Finally, look back at what you have written in this exercise. Where did you choose *be going to* and where did you choose *will*? Why did you make these choices?

Exercise 4

Read the following carefully and decide if the use of *be going to* or *will* is appropriate or not. Check (√) the sentences you think are acceptable. Correct the sentences you think are unacceptable.

1. A: Do you have any plans for tonight?
   B: Yes. We will go to the baseball game. Do you want to come with us?
2. A: Your nephew is a very talented artist, isn't he?
   B: Yes. We believe he'll be very famous one of these days.
3. A: Who do you think will win the next World Cup?
   B: I think Brazil is going to win next time.
   A: Really?
4. A: Where's Freddie?
   B: He will spend the night at his friend's house.
5. A: Have you heard the news? Heidi's going to get married.
   B: That's great!

Focus 5

Be Going To versus Will:
Promises and Willingness

USE

- *Will* is also used to show willingness to do something, often at the moment that the speaker decides to do it:

    (a) A: I think there's someone at the front door.

         B: I'll go and check.

    Will is preferred to *be going to* here because it shows that the speaker has just decided to do something or is willing to do something right away. The contracted *'ll* form is usually used in this case.

- *Will* is also used to make promises:

    (b) I will always love you.

    (c) I'll give you my homework tomorrow, I promise!

Exercise 5

Complete the following, using *be going to*, *'ll*, or *will* as appropriate.

1. A: What are your plans for the weekend?

    B: We _____ take the boat and go fishing.

    A: Sounds great. Can I join you?

2. A: Excuse me, but I can't reach those books on the top shelf.

    B: Move over. I _____ get them down for you.

3. A: You've bought a lot of groceries today.

    B: Yes. I _____ cook dinner for the people who work in my office.

4. A: Here's $20.

    B: Thank you. I promise I _____ pay you back next week.

5. A: Can we have some volunteers to help paint the new homeless shelter?

   B: Harry and I _____ do it. We really want to help.

6. A: Oops! I've just spilled my drink all over everything.

   B: Don't panic. I _____ get a cloth.

7. A: What _____ (you) wear to Aki's party?

   B: Kuniko and I _____ wear jeans. What about you?

8. A: Now, kids, I want you to be very good this afternoon because I'm not feeling well.

   B: It's O.K., Mrs. Swanson. We promise we _____ behave.

9. A: What's up?

   B: I'm late for work and my car won't start.

   A: Don't worry. I _____ give you a ride.

10. A: What _____ (you) do with your brother when he comes to visit next

    weekend?

    B: First, Jody and I _____ take him out to brunch down by the beach, and

    after that Kate _____ show him the sights.

Activities

Activity 1

The purpose of this activity is to collect as much information as possible about the future plans and intentions of your classmates.

Look at the chart below. Your task is to complete as many squares as you can by finding the required information. Write the name or names of the people who gave you the information in the square. "Maybe" and "I don't know" are not acceptable answers! The first person to get a line of three squares—vertically, horizontally or diagonally—is the winner. Good luck!

Find someone who is going to take the TOEFL soon. When is she or he going to take it?	Find three people who are going to cook dinner tonight. What are they going to cook?	Find two people who are going to smoke after this class.
Find two people who are going to play the same sport this week. What sport are they going to play?	Find someone who is going to move to another city within a year. What city is she or he going to move to?	Find someone who is going to go to the movies today. What movie is she or he going to see?
Find someone who is going to get his or her hair cut in the next two weeks.	Find two people who are not going to watch TV this week.	Find two people who are going to celebrate their birthdays next month.

Activity 2

Write fortune cookie "fortunes" for your teachers and five of your classmates. Write each fortune on a small slip of paper, the same size as in real fortune cookies, and give each one to the appropriate person.

Activity 3

What are your predictions for the next ten years? What do you think will happen in the world? What do you think will happen in your country? Write a brief report on your predictions. Your report should include a short introduction to your topic. When you finish writing, read your report carefully and check your use of *will* and *be going to*. Remember, it is often possible to use either one. Remember also that it is not necessary to use *will* and *be going to* in every sentence you write!

We have written the beginning of a report to give you some ideas, but you probably have better ideas of your own.

LIFE IN THE FUTURE

Nobody knows exactly what will happen in the future, but in my opinion, we will see many important changes in the world in the next ten years. Some of them will be good and some of them will be bad. In this short report, I will talk about some of my predictions for the future of the world, as well as the future of my country.

First, let me tell you about my predictions for the world. . . .

Activity 4

In this activity, you will be interviewing young North Americans about their goals and future plans. If possible, try to interview young people at different stages of their lives: college students, high school students, and children. Find out what they are going to do when they leave school. Report your findings to the class.

If possible, tape your interviews. Later listen to your tape and take note of the different ways these native speakers talk about the future. Make a list of the most interesting plans and share them with the rest of the class.

Activity 5

In this activity, you will be creating a chain story about your teacher's next vacation. Your teacher will start by telling you where he or she is going for his or her next vacation and one thing he or she is going to do:

Teacher: I'm going to Hawaii for my vacation, and I am going to climb a mountain.

The next person repeats the first part and adds another statement about the teacher's vacation until everyone in the room has added to the description.

Student 1: (Teacher's name) is going to Hawaii; he or she is going to climb a mountain and he or she is going to swim in the ocean too.

4

Past Progressive and Simple Past with Time Clauses
When, While, and *As Soon As*

Task*

Last night Lewis Meyer died at his home in Miami. Phil Fork, a police detective, was the first person to arrive at the house after Mr. Meyer died. This is what he found:

DUANE GILLOGLY

Mr. Meyer's wife, Margo, told Fork: "It was an accident. My husband took a shower at about 10:00 P.M. After his shower, he slipped on a piece of soap and fell down."

*Based on the situation in "Tragedy in the Bathroom" in *Crime and Puzzlement* by Lawrence Treat, 1935, published by David R. Godine

DO YOU BELIEVE HER?

Look at the picture and work with a partner to decide what happened. Be ready to share your answers with your classmates and to say why you think each statement is true (T) or false (F).

1. Mr. Meyer died after Phil Fork arrived.   T   F
2. Mr. Meyer died when Phil Fork arrived.   T   F
3. Mr. Meyer died before Phil Fork arrived.   T   F
4. Mr. Meyer brushed his teeth before he died.   T   F
5. Mr. Meyer was brushing his teeth when he died.   T   F
6. Mr. Meyer was taking a shower when he died.   T   F
7. Mr. Meyer took a shower before he died.   T   F
8. Mr. Meyer died when he slipped on a piece of soap.   T   F
9. Somebody hit Mr. Meyer over the head while he was brushing his teeth.   T   F
10. The murder weapon is still in the bathroom.   T   F

YOU ARE THE DETECTIVE ... WHAT REALLY HAPPENED?
(You can find the solution to this problem at the end of this unit.)

Focus 1

USE

Past Progressive versus Simple Past

USE

- When we talk about actions or events that **started and finished** in the past, we usually use the simple past:

(a) Ramon left the party at 9:00 last night.

Past   9:00 p.m.   Now
LAST NIGHT

- When we talk about an action that **was in progress** at a specific time in the past, we use the past progressive:

(b) Ramon was leaving the party at 9:00 last night.

Past   9:00 p.m.   Now
LAST NIGHT

- We often use the past progressive with the simple past to describe two actions in the past:
  (c) Ramon was leaving the party when I arrived.

LAST NIGHT

- The past progressive refers to an action that was in progress when something else happened. It started before this time and possibly continued after it.

Focus 2

FORM

Form of the Past Progressive

FORM

- *was/were* + verb + *-ing*

Statement	Negative	Question
I She He It } **was sleeping.**	I She He It } **was not sleeping.** **(wasn't)**	**Was** { I she he it } **sleeping?**
We You They } **were sleeping.**	We You They } **were not sleeping.** **(weren't)**	**Were** { we you they } **sleeping?**

Exercise 1

Complete this newspaper report of Mr. Meyer's murder without turning back to the Task.

DAILY NEWS

BATHROOM MURDER

"I am innocent!" says Mrs. Meyer.

Last night police arrested Margo Meyer for the murder of her husband, Lewis. On her way to the police station, Mrs. Meyer told reporters: "I am innocent. I loved my husband very much. I didn't kill him."

According to Mrs Meyer, on the night of his

death, her husband _____

_____

when _____

_____ .

However, Detective Phil Fork believes _____

_____

while _____

_____ .

Focus 3

MEANING

When, While, and *As Soon As*

MEANING

- *While, when,* and *as soon as* are time adverbials. *While* is associated with an action in progress. It means "during that time":

  (a) While I was reading the newspaper, Donald called.

- *When* is associated with a completed action. It means "at that time":

  (b) When Donald called, I was reading the newspaper.

  However, *when* and *while* are often used in the same way. *When* is more common, and we often use it in place of *while*, especially in informal situations.

- *As soon as* is also associated with a completed action. It means "immediately after":

  (c) As soon as we heard the good news, we started to celebrate.

Exercise 2

Make meaningful statements about Mr. Meyer's murder by matching information from A with information from B. The first one has been done for you.

A	B
1. Mrs. Meyer called the police	she insisted she was innocent.
2. While she was waiting for the police to arrive	as soon as he arrived.
3. As soon as Phil Fork heard about the murder	when her husband died.
4. Mrs. Meyer took him to the scene of the crime	while the police were taking her to jail.
5. While Phil Fork was searching the bathroom for clues	while he was brushing his teeth.
6. He saw that Mr. Meyer died	she placed a bar of soap on the bathroom floor.
7. When Phil Fork charged Mrs. Meyer with murder	he rushed to the Meyer's house.
8. A crowd of news reporters tried to interview Mrs. Meyer	he became suspicious of Mrs. Meyer's story.

Exercise 3

Look again at the sentences you created in Exercise 2. For each one, underline the part of the sentence that gives information about time. This is the part of the sentence that answers the question "When?" For example: He saw that Mr. Meyer died <u>while he was brushing his teeth.</u>

Focus 4

FORM

Time Clauses with *When, While,* and *As Soon As*

 FORM

- Time clauses answer the question "When?" by giving information about the time an action or event happened. They contain a subject and a verb and are introduced by time terms like *when, while,* and *as soon as*:

  (a) **While Renata was crossing the street,** she ran into her ex-boyfriend.

  (b) We left **as soon as we got your phone call.**

  (c) **When Phyllis arrived home,** everyone rushed out to greet her.

- A time clause is a dependent clause; this means that it is not complete by itself. For example, in order to fully understand, *When Phyllis arrived home*, we need more information. A time clause therefore depends on the rest of the sentence (the independent or main clause) to complete its meaning:

  Dependent Time Clause   **Main (Independent) Clause**
  (d) **When Phyllis arrived home,** everybody rushed out to greet her.
- A time clause can come at the beginning of a sentence:

  (e) **While my father was cooking the dinner**, our guests arrived.
- A time clause can also come at the end:

  (f) Our guests arrived **while my father was cooking the dinner**.
- If the time clause comes at the beginning of the sentence, use a comma between the time clause and the main clause:

  When _____ , _____ .
  (time clause)   (comma)   (main clause)

  While _____ , _____ .
  (time clause)   (comma)   (main clause)

  As soon as _____ , _____ .
  (time clause)   (comma)   (main clause)
- If the main clause comes at the beginning of the sentence and the time clause comes last, do not use a comma between the two clauses:

  _____ when _____ .
  (main clause)   (time clause)

  _____ while _____ .
  (main clause)   (time clause)

  _____ as soon as _____ .
  (main clause)   (time clause)

Exercise 4

Turn back to the sentences you created in Exercise 2. Write them below and add punctuation, as necessary.

1. _____

2. _____

3. _____

4. _____

5. _____

6. _____

7. _____

8. _____

Exercise 5

Work with a partner and write down five things you know about John Lennon.

1. _____ .

2. _____ .

3. _____ .

4. _____ .

5. _____ .

Here is some more information about John Lennon's life. The wavy line (⁓⁓⁓) indicates an action in progress. X indicates a completed action.

1. attend high school ⁓⁓⁓⁓⁓⁓⁓⁓⁓⁓⁓⁓ _____ X his mother dies	2. attend high school ⁓⁓⁓⁓⁓⁓⁓⁓⁓⁓⁓⁓ _____ X meet Paul McCartney
3. study at art school ⁓⁓⁓⁓⁓⁓⁓⁓⁓⁓⁓⁓ _____ X form The Beatles	4. perform in clubs ⁓⁓⁓⁓⁓⁓⁓⁓⁓⁓⁓⁓ in Liverpool ⁓⁓⁓⁓⁓⁓⁓⁓⁓⁓ _____ X sign his first recording contract
5. live in London ⁓⁓⁓⁓⁓⁓⁓⁓⁓⁓ _____ X fall in love with Yoko Ono	6. work for peace and ⁓⁓⁓⁓⁓⁓⁓⁓⁓⁓⁓⁓ write new songs ⁓⁓⁓⁓⁓⁓⁓⁓⁓⁓ _____ X die
7. leave his apartment ⁓⁓⁓⁓⁓⁓⁓⁓⁓⁓ _____ X one of his fans shoots him	

Use this information to finish the short biography below. Fill in the blanks, using simple past or past progressive. The first one has been done for you as an example.

John Lennon was one of the most famous singer/songwriters of his time. He was born in Liverpool, England, in 1940, but his childhood was not very happy. (1) *His mother died* while *he was attending high school.* Life was difficult for John after his mother's death, but after a time things got better. (2) _____ while _____ .

Soon Paul introduced him to George Harrison, and they began to play in a band together. After that, John left high school and became an art student. (3) While _____ .

Soon after John formed the Beatles, he married his first wife, Cynthia, and they had a son, Julian. (4) _____ when _____ .

John and the Beatles moved to London and became very famous throughout the world. (5) _____ while _____ . A couple of years later, the Beatles split up. John and Yoko got married and they moved to the United States, where their son Sean was born. John (6) _____ when _____ . On December 8, 1980, (7) _____ while _____ . John Lennon died many years ago, but he still has many fans all over the world.

Exercise 6

Complete the sentences in the story below using the word in parentheses. Decide whether you should use simple past or past progressive.

NOTE: *After* and *before* also introduce time clauses, but we use them with the simple past tense only, in contrast to *while* and *when*.

1. Yesterday morning at 10:00, Marie _____ (go) to see the dentist.

2. While she _____ (wait) for her appointment, her old friend

   Lin _____ (come) into the dentist's waiting room.

3. Before Marie _____ (get) her new job at the software company, she and Lin

   _____ (work) together at the bank.

4. When Marie and Lin _____ (see) each other in the waiting room, they

   _____ (be) surprised and delighted.

5. They _____ (realize) that they had not seen each other for several months.

6. While they _____ (wait) for their appointments, they _____ (talk

   and laugh) about old times.

7. When it _____ (be) finally time for Marie to see the dentist, they _____

   (not + want) to stop talking.

8. Just before Marie _____ (leave) the waiting room, they _____

   (make) a date to to see each other again.

9. While Marie _____ (leave) the waiting room, Lin _____ (say), "I

   hope you don't have any cavities!"

Exercise 7

Combine the two sentences below into one sentence. Use the time word on the left to make a time clause and put the verb into simple past or past progressive.

1. (as soon as) Event #1: I (finish) shopping for groceries.
                 Event #2: I (drive) home.

   EXAMPLE: *As soon as I finished shopping for groceries, I drove home.*

                OR

                I drove home as soon as I finished shopping for groceries.

2. (when)   Event #1: I (get) home
                Event #2: I (put) the groceries away.

3. (as soon as) Event #1: I (finish) my homework.
                Event #2: I (make) dinner.

4. (while)   Event #1: I (make) dinner.
                Event #2: My roommate (come) home.

5. (when)   Event #1: I (ask) my roommate if he was hungry.
                Event #2: He got upset.

6. (while)   Event #1:   My roommate (explain) why he was upset.

                    Event #2:   I (load) his plate with food.

7. (when)   Event #1:   He (look) down at the food on his plate.

                    Event #2:   He (calm) down.

8. (as soon as) Event #1:   He (start) to eat.

                    Event #2:   He (apologize) to me.

Activities

Activity 1

Nan Silviera has just written her first book:

About the author:

Nan Silviera graduated from Arizona State University in 1975. In 1976, she sailed across the Pacific single-handedly. After that, she.........

....
....
....
....

JOURNEYS

by
Nan Silviera

     As you can see, the author's life story on the back of the book is not complete. Work with a partner to finish writing it.

     Student A is to turn to page 43 and Student B is to turn to page 45. You both have information about Nan's life, but some of the information is missing. Do not show your books to each other, but ask each other questions to get information about the parts marked "?". Write down the information your partner gives you so that when you finish, you will have the complete story.

     Finally, use the information from your chart to write about Nan's life. You can use the biography on the back of her book to begin your story. When you finish writing, check your work to see if you have used time adverbials and the past progressive and past simple tenses appropriately.

Activity 2

In this activity, you will be finding information about your classmates' lives by asking about what they were doing at the times below. In the last box, add a time of your own choice.

Do not write information about yourself; go around the room and get as much information from as many different people as possible. Write the information in the boxes on the right. Be ready to share the most interesting or surprising information you find with the rest of the class.

TIME	
at 8:30 P.M. last Saturday	
in May 1989	
five hours ago	
ten years ago today	

Activity 3

Take a large sheet of paper and make a time line for your own life like the one in Activity 1. Bring your time line to class and describe the story of your life to your classmates.

Activity 4

The death of President Kennedy in 1963 was an enormous shock to Americans and to people all over the world. Most Americans who were alive at that time can remember exactly what they were doing when they heard the news of Kennedy's assassination. Interview at least three people who were alive at that time (you will probably have to find people over 35!) and find out what they were doing when they heard the news of Kennedy's death. Share your findings with the rest of the class. If possible, tape-record your interviews. Listen carefully to your recording and note if the speakers use any of the structures discussed in this unit.

A

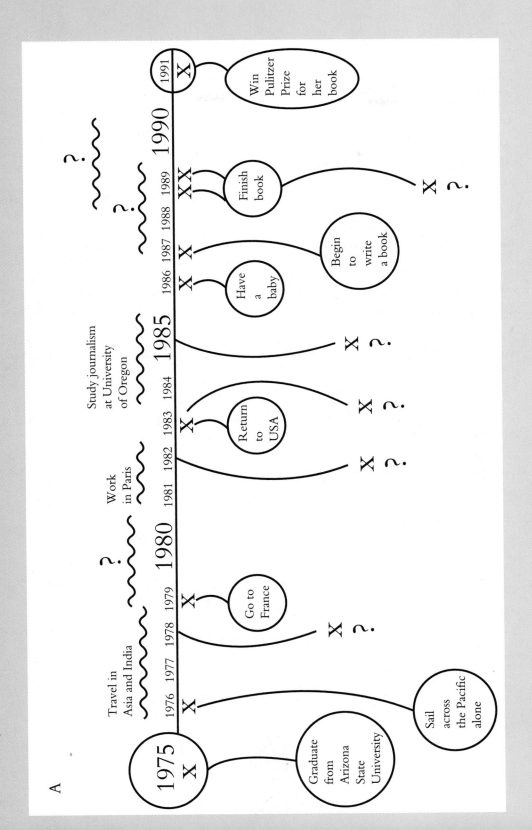

Activity 5

Alibi

An alibi is a story that proves a person did not commit a crime because she or he was at a different place at the time of the crime.

A crime was committed around 10:00 P.M. last night. The purpose of this team game is to create an alibi for your team and to "break" the alibis of the other teams in the game.

Divide into teams of three or four people. You have five minutes to get together with your team to create an alibi for what you were all doing together between 9:00 P.M. and midnight last night. Try to agree on as many details as possible. For example, what were you doing? Where were you doing it? What were you wearing?

When everyone is ready, the first team goes out of the room. The rest of the class are now police detectives, and your job is to question the team one by one to see if they can keep to the same alibi. Call one person back into the room and ask questions about what she or he was doing. Keep notes of the answers. Next, call the second person into the room and ask *the same questions*. If she or he gives a different answer to any of the questions, his or her team must drop out of the game. (The rest of the team can now come back into the room and become police detectives.) The winning team is the team that keeps to the same story. Good luck.

Solution to the Task

Mrs. Meyer killed her husband. She entered the bathroom while he was brushing his teeth, and she hit him over the head with the bathroom scale. Then she turned on the shower and put the soap on the floor.

How Do We Know This?

From the toothbrush: He was brushing his teeth, not walking from the shower.

From the footprints: We can see his wife went into the shower.

From the soap: It was not possible to slip in this position.

From the bathroom scale: The scale does not indicate zero.

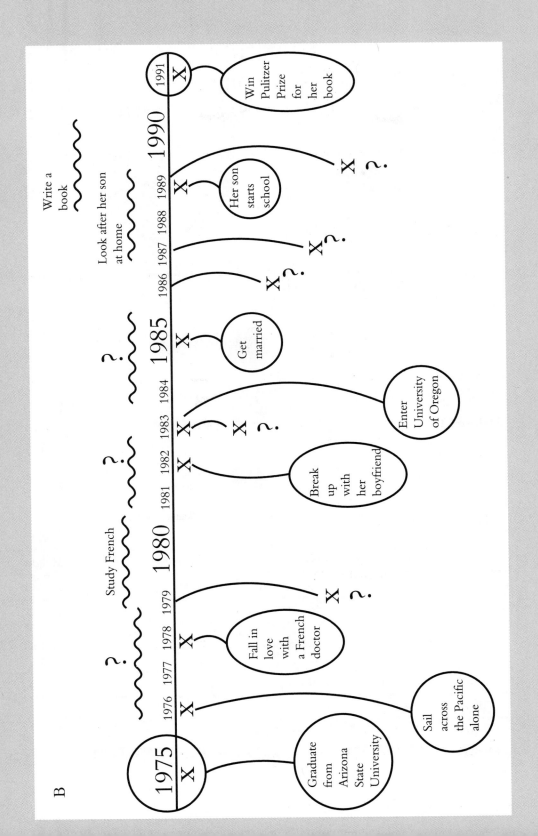

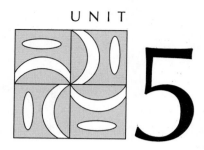

UNIT 5

Similarities and Differences
Comparatives, Superlatives, Equatives, and Negative Equatives

Task

The silhouettes in this picture are from a photograph of a group of friends. Use the information from the chart and the list of clues to identify each person. Write their names in the correct position on the picture.

THE LEFT   THE RIGHT

Name	Likes	Age	Hair	Occupation	Eyes	Height
LINDA	football	75	red	doctor	green	5'9 1/2"
BOB	beer	19	brown	student	blue	5'9 1/2"
SUSAN	music	25	blonde	student	green	5'1"
FRANK	cats	43	gray	artist	brown	6'4"
CARLA	food	28	black	singer	blue	5'5"
GEORGE	movies	44	bald	writer	brown	5'10"
DIANA	opera	58	brown	engineer	gray	5'10"

CLUES

1. The oldest person is behind the youngest woman.
2. The tallest woman is behind someone who is thirty years younger than her.
3. The shortest person is in front of someone with green eyes.
4. The tallest man is next to the tallest woman.
5. The person who likes beer is not quite as tall as the person next to him on the right.
6. The man who is on the right of the youngest person is behind the tallest person.
7. The youngest person is as tall as the person next to him on the left.
8. The 28-year-old singer is not next to anybody.

When you finish, check your answers with the rest of the class to see if you all agree. You can find the solution to the Task at the end of the unit.

Focus 1

Expressing Difference: Comparatives and Superlatives

FORM
MEANING

- One of the most common ways of expressing difference is through the use of comparatives and superlatives.
  - Superlatives express **extremes** of difference among people or things:

   (a) Susan **is the shortest,** and Frank **is the tallest.**

- Comparatives show relative differences among people or things, but they do not show the extremes of difference:

   (b) George **is taller than** Linda.
   (c) Carla **is shorter than** George.

- Comparatives and superlatives can be used with all parts of speech:

		Comparative	Superlative
Adjectives			
One Syllable	young	young**er than**	**the** young**est**
One Syllable + -*y*	easy	eas**ier than**	**the** eas**iest**
Two or More Syllables	difficult	**more** difficult **than** **less** difficult **than**	**the most** difficult **the least** difficult
Adverbs	carefully	**more** carefully **than** **less** carefully **than**	**the most** carefully **the least** carefully
Verbs	weigh	weigh **more than** weigh **less than**	weigh **the most** weigh **the least**
Nouns	money	**more** money **than** **less** money **than**	**the most** money **the least** money

Exercise 1

First fill in the blanks or complete the words and then use the information from the Task to decide if the statements are true (T) or false (F).

1. The oldest woman is taller __ __ __ __ the oldest man.   T   F

2. George is tall __ __ than the person beside him.   T   F

3. Diana is young __ __   __ __ __ __ __ the man beside her on the right.   T   F

4. George is tall __ __   __ __ __ __ Frank.   T   F

5. The singer is several years older __ __ __ __ the person behind her.   T   F

6. The doctor is __ __ __ old __ __ __ .   T   F

7. Bob is old __ __   __ __ __ __ the person in front of him.   T   F

8. The young __ __ __ woman is in front of __ __ __ old __ __ __ woman.   T   F

9. Frank is __ __ __ tall __ __ __ man, but he isn't __ __ __ old __ __ __ .   T   F

10. __ __ __ old __ __ __ man is short __ __   __ __ __ __ __ __ __

   young __ __ __ woman.   T   F

Focus 2

FORM ● MEANING

Degrees of Similarity and Difference

FORM
MEANING

- Expressing similarity:
  - To express similarity between people or things, you can use an **equative** *(as . . . as)*:

(a)	Linda is 5′9 1/2″.	Linda is **as tall as** Bob.
(b)	Bob is 5′9 1/2″.	OR Bob is **as tall as** Linda.

- To emphasize the amount of similarity, you can add: *exactly, almost, nearly, not quite, just about,* or *practically:*

(c)	George is 5′10″.	George is **exactly as tall as** Diana.
(d)	Diana is 5′10″.	OR Diana is **exactly as tall as** George.

(e) George is 5′10″.

(f) Bob is 5′9 1/2″.

Bob is { almost / nearly / not quite / practically / just about } **as tall as** George.

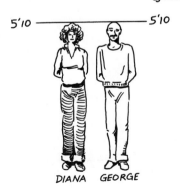

49

- Expressing difference:
  - Another way to express difference is by using a negative **equative** *(not as . . . as)*:
    (g) George is 5'10".   Bob is **not as tall as** George.
    (h) Bob is 5'9 1/2".
  - You can emphasize the amount of difference by adding *not nearly, nowhere near, not anywhere near:*

    (i) Susan is 5'1".
    (j) Diana is 5'10".

    Susan is $\left\{\begin{array}{l}\textbf{not nearly}\\ \textbf{nowhere near}\\ \textbf{not anywhere near}\end{array}\right\}$ **as tall as** Diana.

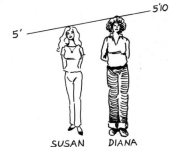

- *Nowhere near as* and *not anywhere near as* are colloquial and are only used in conversation and informal speech.

Exercise 2

Use the information in the Task to complete the following, using the appropriate equatives, comparatives, or superlatives. Show the amount of difference or similarity as necessary.

1. Linda/Bob/height

   Linda is as tall as Bob .

2. Susan/Frank/height

   _____ .

3. Linda/Diana/height

   _____ .

4. Linda/Carla/height

   _____ .

5. George/Susan/height and age

   _____ .

6. Bob/George/height

   _____ .

7. Frank/George/age

_____

8. Diana/Linda/age

_____

9. Frank/height

_____

10. Linda/age

_____

11. George/Diana/height

_____

How many more meaningful comparisons can you make using the chart in the Task?

Focus 3

FORM

How to Use Equatives and Negative Equatives

FORM

- Like comparatives and superlatives, equatives and negative equatives can be used with all parts of speech:

Adjectives	(a) Susan is not as **tall** as Carla.
Adverbs	(b) Frank does not work as **quickly** as George.
Nouns	(c) Linda does not have as much **money** as Diana. (d) Diana does not have as many **friends** as Carla.
Verbs	(e) George **works** as much as Linda.

- *As* can be followed by:

Clauses	(f) Susan works as hard as **Carla works.** (g) Carla is not as tall as **Linda is.**
Reduced Clauses	(h) Susan works as hard as Carla **does.**
Noun Phrases	(i) Susan works as hard as **Carla.** (j) Carla is not as tall as **Linda.**
Subject Pronouns	(k) Susan works as hard as **I/you/he/she/we/they.**

- Subject pronouns are rarely used, except in very formal situations. Reduced clauses are generally preferred to subject pronouns by themselves:

  (l) Susan works as hard as **I do.**
  - Object Pronouns:

    (m) Susan works as hard as **me/you/her/him/us/them.**
- Object pronouns are very common in conversation and informal writing.
  - Possessive Pronouns:

    (n) Susan's hair is not as short as **mine**.
  - Notice the change in meaning:

(o) Susan's hair is as long as me:

SUSAN'S HAIR   ME

(p) Susan's hair is as long as mine:

SUSAN'S HAIR   MY HAIR

Exercise 3

Correct the mistakes in the following sentences.

1. All her life, Hester has been lucky than her sister, Miriam.
2. Hester is not intelligent as Miriam but she was always more successful than Miriam in school.
3. For example, Hester's grades were always better than Miriam.
4. Both sisters are pretty, but many people believe that Miriam is prettier that her sister.
5. However, Miriam does not have as much boyfriends as her sister does.
6. They both have excellent jobs, but Miriam thinks her job isn't as interesting as her sister.
7. They both travel as part of their work, but Hester goes to more exciting places than Miriam is.
8. In spite of these differences, Miriam thinks that she is happier that her sister is.
9. However, Hester knows that she is lucky and she thinks that good luck is as important than good looks and intelligence.

Exercise 4

Work in a group to create a problem like the one in the Task. First use the picture and blank chart to record your information and then write the clues. Each clue must contain at least one of the following: a comparative; a superlative; an equative; a negative equative. Finally, exchange your problem with another group and see if you can solve each other's problems.

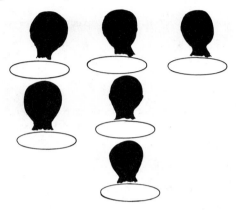

Name	Age	Height	Occupation	Likes

CLUES

_____

_____

_____

_____

Focus 4

Making Tactful Comparisons

USE

- Many of the adjectives that we use in comparisons express opposite meanings. These are called *polarity* or *opposite* adjectives:

tall	large	short	small
old	fast	young	slow
("MORE")		("LESS")	

- In general, the adjectives that express "more" are considered neutral because they do not give any special emphasis to the meaning of the adjective. For example, we usually ask:

  How **old** are you?

  NOT: How **young** are you?

  We only ask, "How young are you?" when we want to give special emphasis to *young*.

- To make comparisons using *as . . . as* and *not as . . . as,* we also usually choose the neutral adjective. For example:

  (a) Linda is **as tall as** Bob.

  (a) is neutral; we think only about Bob's and Linda's height. However, (b) draws attention to *short*, and we understand that both Bob and Linda are especially short.

  (b) Linda is **as short as** Bob.

  (c) Patricia is **as old as** Virginia. (Neutral)

  (d) Patricia is **as young as** Virginia. (Emphasis is on *young*.)

- The following statements express the same meaning:

  (e) Bob is **not as tall as** Frank.

  (f) Frank is **not as short as** Bob.

  (g) Frank is **not as short as** Bob.

BOB   FRANK

  However, (e) is more positive about Bob's height. (f) emphasizes the difference between Frank and Bob and suggests that Bob is especially short. If Bob is sensitive about his height, it is more tactful to choose the neutral adjective.

- Therefore, when you know someone may be sensitive about the comparison you wish to make, you can use **not as . . . as + a neutral opposite adjective.** You can also use **not quite as** to soften the comparison and minimize the difference even more:

  (h) Otis is **not quite as bright as** Rocky.

  (i) His latest book is **not quite as good as** his earlier ones.

Exercise 5

Your boss has asked you to act as interpreter at an important business meeting with some foreign clients. He would like to do business with these clients, but there are some problems to be discussed because the two companies are very different. Unfortunately, your boss is very direct, and you believe that some of his statements will probably offend the clients.

Change his statements so that they will be less direct and more tactful. Use the adjectives in parentheses with *not as . . . as*. Add *not quite* if you want to be even more tactful. The first one has been done for you:

1. Your company is smaller than ours. (large)

   Your <u>company is not as large as ours</u>_____.

2. Your factories are more old-fashioned than ours. (modern)

   Your _____.

3. Your workers are lazier than ours. (energetic)

   Your _____.

4. Your products are less popular than ours. (well known)

   Your _____.

5. Our advertising is more successful than yours. (effective)

   Your _____.

6. Your designs are more conservative than ours. (up to date)

   Your _____.

7. Your production is slower than ours. (fast)

   Your _____.

8. The quality of your product line is lower than ours. (high)

   The _____.

9. Your factories are dirtier than ours. (clean)

   Your _____.

10. Your factories are more dangerous than ours. (safe)

    Your _____.

Exercise 6

Omar is president of the international students' association at an American college located in a small town in the midwest. The chamber of commerce has asked him to give a speech to local businessmen on foreign students' reactions to life in America. He has made a survey of the foreign students on campus, and he is using the results of the survey for his speech. Some of the comments are not very complimentary, but he feels the local community should know what foreign students really think. He therefore decides to edit some of the more direct comments so that they will be informative but not offensive. He is having problems with the following. Can you help?

1. In America, people are less sincere.

   _____.

2. People in my country are much friendlier and are more hospitable.

   _____.

3. Americans are often very rude; people in my country are never rude.

   _____.

4. The cities here are dirtier and more dangerous than at home.

   _____.

5. Americans are lazy compared to people in my country.

   _____.

6. American food is tasteless compared to the food in my country.

   _____.

7. The nightlife in this town is really boring compared to the nightlife at home.

   _____.

8. People here watch too much television. We watch much less TV at home.

   _____.

Do you agree or disagree with these comments?
Do you have any comments of your own that Omar could include in his speech? Add them here:

Activities

Activity 1

Write a brief guide for American families who want to become host families for students from your country. What should American host families know about the differences between your culture and customs and those of the United States? Be tactful where necessary!

Activity 2

There are many common idioms in English that use the construction *as . . . as.*

Here are some common ones:

as stubborn as a mule

as happy as a clam

as strong as an ox

Interview several native speakers and ask them to tell you as many of these idioms as they can remember. Find out what they mean and share your findings with the rest of the class.

Idiom	Meaning
as ——————— as ———————	

Activity 3

Get together with another student. Observe him or her quietly for one minute and then write down all the similarities and all the differences between you that you can think of. Compare your lists. How many of your differences and similarities were the same? Together, can you think of any more? Share your findings with the rest of the class.

Activity 4

Go through as many newspapers and magazines as possible and clip all the examples of different types of comparisons that you can find (in headlines, advertisements, and so on). Bring these to class and get together with a group of three or four other students. Make a "Comparison Poster," using the examples you found. Share your posters with the rest of the class.

Solution to the Task

LINDA   BOB   GEORGE
SUSAN   DIANA   FRANK
        CARLA

UNIT 6

Degree Complements

Too, Enough, Very

Task

Mary is looking for a place to rent. She is looking for a two-bedroom house or apartment with lots of light and plenty of closet space. She cannot pay more than $800 a month. She read the classified ads in the newspaper and went to see the following places. She also made notes on each place she saw. Can you match her notes to the appropriate classified ad? Which one do you think she probably chose?

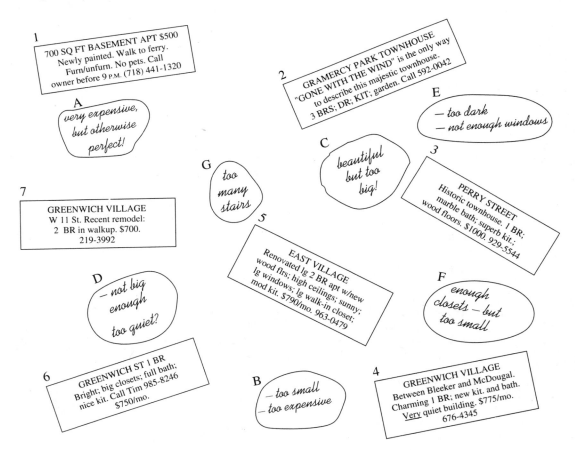

1
700 SQ FT BASEMENT APT $500
Newly painted. Walk to ferry.
Furn/unfurn. No pets. Call
owner before 9 P.M. (718) 441-1320

A
very expensive, but otherwise perfect!

2
GRAMERCY PARK TOWNHOUSE
"GONE WITH THE WIND" is the only way
to describe this majestic townhouse.
3 BRS; DR; KIT; garden. Call 592-0042

E
— too dark
— not enough windows

C
beautiful but too big!

G
too many stairs

3
PERRY STREET
Historic townhouse. 1 BR;
marble bath; superb kit.;
wood floors. $1000. 929-5544

7
GREENWICH VILLAGE
W 11 St. Recent remodel:
2 BR in walkup. $700.
219-3992

5
EAST VILLAGE
Renovated lg 2 BR apt w/new
wood flrs; high ceilings; sunny;
lg windows; lg walk-in closet;
mod kit. $790/mo. 963-0479

D
— not big enough
too quiet?

F
enough closets — but too small

6
GREENWICH ST 1 BR
Bright; big closets; full bath;
nice kit. Call Tim 985-8246
$750/mo.

B
— too small
— too expensive

4
GREENWICH VILLAGE
Between Bleeker and McDougal.
Charming 1 BR; new kit. and bath.
Very quiet building. $775/mo.
676-4345

58

Focus 1

Expressing Sufficiency, Insufficiency, and Excess

MEANING

- *Enough* expresses sufficiency; it shows you have as much as you need and that you do not need any more:

    (a) There are **enough** closets.

    (b) The apartment is big **enough** for both of us.

    Enough suggests a positive feeling about the situation.

- *Not enough* expresses insufficiency; it shows you do not have all that is necessary or desirable for doing something:

    (c) There are **not enough** windows in this apartment. (I want more windows.)

    (d) The bedroom is **not** big **enough.** (I want a bigger bedroom.)

    Not enough suggests a negative feeling about the situation.

- *Too* expresses excess (more than you want or need) or insufficiency (less than you want or need), depending on the meaning of the word that follows:

    (e) The rent is **too** high. (EXCESS: The rent is **more** than I want to pay.)

    (f) The kitchen is **too** small. (INSUFFICIENCY: It is less than I want; I want something bigger.)

    In both contexts, *too* suggests a negative feeling about the situation:

    (g) This coffee is **too** hot. (I can't drink it.)

    (h) He speaks **too** quickly. (I can't understand him.)

    (i) She is **too** young to drink. (She can't drink alcohol here.)

Exercise 1

Can you find an appropriate cause for the following problems?

PROBLEM	CAUSE
1. My feet really hurt.	You don't go to the dentist often enough.
2. I'm broke!	Maybe you shouted too much at the ball game.
3. I failed my math test.	You didn't add enough salt.
4. I've gained a lot of weight recently.	Perhaps your shoes aren't big enough.
5. I never feel hungry at mealtimes.	You spend too much money.
6. I can't sleep at night.	Your stereo is too loud.
7. I have a sore throat.	You don't get enough exercise.
8. This soup is tasteless.	You eat too many snacks.
9. My neighbors are always angry with me.	You drink too much coffee.
10. My teeth hurt.	You didn't study enough.

Focus 2

FORM

How to Use *Enough, Not Enough,* and *Too*

FORM

- Enough
  - *Enough* follows adjectives, adverbs, and verbs:
    - **(a)** This house is **big enough.**   This house is **not big enough.**
    - **(b)** He speaks **clearly enough.**   He does **not** speak **clearly enough.**
    - **(c)** We **have seen enough.**   We **have not seen enough.**
    - **(d)** She **ate enough.**   She **did not eat enough.**
  - *Enough* precedes nouns:
    - **(e)** We have **enough money.**   We **do not** have **enough money.**
    - **(f)** There are **enough people** here.   There **are not enough people** here.

- *Enough* can be used with an adjective, adverb, verb, or noun followed by an infinitive.
  - **Adjective + infinitive:**
    (g) She is **old enough to vote.**   She is **not old enough to vote.**
  - **Adverb + infinitive:**
    (h) They studied **hard enough to**   They **didn't** study **hard enough to**
        pass the test.   **pass** the test.
  - **Verb + infinitive:**
    (i) We **earned enough to buy** a   We **didn't earn enough to buy** a
        new car.   new car.
  - **Noun + infinitive:**
    (j) I have **enough chocolate to** make a   I don't have **enough chocolate to**
        cake.   **make** a cake.
- Too
  - *Too* precedes adjectives and adverbs:
    (k) She is **too young.**
    (l) They work **too slowly.**
  - *Too* + adjective is often followed by an infinitive:
    (m) This tea is **too hot to drink.**
    (n) We were **too tired to stay** at the party.
  - *Too* + adjective is often followed by *for* + noun / pronoun + infinitive:
    (o) The book was **too difficult for him to understand.**
    (p) He walked **too fast for the children to keep up.**

Exercise 2

Complete the following appropriately, using *too, enough,* or *not enough* as necessary. There are many different ways to make meaningful responses in this exercise. Compare your answers with a partner and see how many different responses you can make.

1. A: Why are you wearing so many sweaters?

   B: Because this room *is too cold / isn't warm enough.*

2. A: Does your brother have a car?

   B: No, he's only 14! He's _____.

3. A: Why did they move?

   B: They're expecting a baby, and their old house_____.

4. A: Would you like some more pie?

   B: No, thanks. It's delicious, but I _____.

5. A: Can we count on your support in next month's election?

   B: I'm sorry, but I _____ . I won't be 18 until next year.

6. A: What's wrong?

   B: My jeans _____ . I can't get them on.

   A: Why don't you buy a new pair?

   B: I don't get paid until next week, so I _____ .

7. A: Waiter!

   B: Yes, sir?

   A: We can't eat this. It _____ .

8. A: Let me help you carry that.

   B: Thanks. This suitcase _____ .

Focus 3

FORM ● MEANING

Too Much and *Too Many;* *Too Little* and *Too Few*

FORM
MEANING

- *Too + much* is used with non-count nouns:
  (a) Jack has **too much money**.
- *Too + many* is used with count nouns:
  (b) There are **too many students** in this class.

  Too much and *too many* express excess, and suggest a negative feeling about the situation.

- *Too + little* is used with non-count nouns:
  (c) There is **too little time** to finish this.
- *Too + few* is used with count nouns:
  (d) The class was canceled because **too few students** enrolled.

  Too few and *too little* express insufficiency, and therefore suggest a negative feeling about the situation.

Exercise 3

Read the following and underline all the expressions or phrases that express the idea of insufficiency. Where possible, replace these with *too little* or *too few* as appropriate and change the verbs as necessary.

My sister's wedding was a disaster. First of all, she decided to get married very suddenly, so there
was too little time
wasn't enough time to plan it properly. Nevertheless, about 50 of her friends came to the reception in her

studio. Unfortunately, there wasn't enough room for everyone, so it was rather uncomfortable. She only

had a few chairs, and our 96-year-old grandmother had to sit on the floor. My father had ordered lots of

champagne, but there weren't enough glasses, so some people didn't get very much to drink. In addition,

we had several problems with the caterers. There wasn't enough cake for everyone, but there was too much

soup! We also had problems with the entertainment. My sister loves Latin music, so she hired a salsa band;

however, it was hard to move in such a small space, and my sister got upset when not enough people wanted

to dance. I got into trouble too. I was the official photographer, but I didn't bring enough film with me, so

now my sister is mad because she only has about ten wedding photographs—and all of them are pictures of

people trying to find a place to sit down!

Focus 4

MEANING
Too versus *Very*

MEANING

(a)   *We often see him.*   This writing is small.

(b)   *She usually doesn't call us.*   This writing is very small.

(c)   *They will arrive tomorrow around midnight.*   This writing is too small.

- *Very* adds emphasis, but *too* shows that something is excessive or more than enough. In (b) the writing is small, but I can read it; however, in (c) I cannot read the writing. Therefore, *too* suggests that you are unable to do something, but *very* does not.

Exercise 4

Complete the following with *too, too + to,* or *very* as appropriate.

1. A: Are you really going to buy that motorcycle?

   B: Yes. It's <u>very</u> expensive, but I think I've got enough money in the bank.

2. A: Why aren't you drinking your tea?

   B: I can't. It's _____ hot _____ drink.

3. A: Can I borrow your truck when I move to my new apartment?

   B: Sure.

   A: Thanks! My car is _____ small _____ carry all my stuff.

4. A: Can you turn your stereo down?

   B: Why?

   A: It's _____ loud! We've been trying to get to sleep for about an hour.

5. A: Do you need some help?

   B: No, thanks. This is _____ heavy, but I think I can manage by myself.

6. A: What do you think of Pat's new boyfriend?

   B: He's _____ quiet, but I like him.

7. A: We haven't heard from you for ages.

   B: I'm sorry. I've been _____ busy _____ call.

8. A: Did you like the movie?

   B: No, it was _____ long.

9. A: Do you want to go home now?

   B: No, not yet. I'm _____ tired, but I think I'll stay a little longer.

10. A: How's the water in the pool?

    B: It's _____ cold! I'm getting out right now.

11. A: Did Brian have fun at the party?

    B: Yes. He seemed to enjoy it _____ much.

12. A: Did Mary decide to rent that apartment?

    B: No, it was _____ small.

Exercise 5

Complete the following with *very, too, too + to, enough, not enough,* or *too much/many/little/few* as appropriate.

Dear Tom and Wendy,

I'm writing to answer your questions about life in in New York. In fact, this is quite hard to do because my opinions keep changing!

My apartment is nice, but the rent is (1) *very*_____ high. Luckily, I earn a good salary and I can afford it. The main problem is that the apartment just is (2) _____ big _____ . I had to sell about half my furniture because I didn't have (3) _____ room for everything. I can't invite people for dinner because the kitchen is (4) _____ small _____ eat in! Luckily, the apartment has lots of windows, so all my plants are getting (5) _____ light. I live (6) _____ close to a subway station; it only takes me a couple of minutes to walk there. However, I never take the subway to work because it's (7) _____ crowded. You wouldn't believe it! There are just (8) _____ people crammed in like sardines, and you can't breathe because there is (9) _____ air. I haven't had the courage to ride my bike yet because there's just (10) _____ traffic. Mostly I walk everywhere, so the good news is that I am getting (11) _____ exercise!

Despite all this, there are lots of wonderful things about living here. There are (12) _____ museums and art galleries to keep me happy for years! However, at the moment, I have (13) _____ time to enjoy them because my job is driving me crazy! It's impossible to get all the work done because there are (14) _____ projects and (15) _____ good people to work on them. As a result, I am (16) _____ busy to make new friends or meet people. I don't sleep (17) _____ , and so I am always tired. Worst of all, I don't even have (18) _____ time to stay in touch with dear old friends like you! Nevertheless, I'm certain things will get better soon. Why don't you come and visit? That would really cheer me up!

Love,

Mary

Activities

Activity 1

Work with a partner or in teams to play this version of tic-tac-toe.

1. Decide who will be "X" and who will be "O" and toss a coin to see who will start the game.
2. For each round of the game, select a different topic from the list below.
3. Choose the square you want to start with. With your team, agree on a meaningful sentence expressing the idea written in the square and relating to the topic of the round. For example: TOPIC: This classroom. "This classroom is very small," "There aren't enough chairs in this classroom," "There are too few windows in this classroom," and so on.
4. The first team to get a line is the winner.

TOPICS

1. This campus
2. Television
3. The United States
4. This town or city

very	enough	too
too few	not enough	too much
not enough	too many	too little

Activity 2

First, look at the chart below. If you were responsible for making the laws in your community, at what ages would you permit the following activities? Write these in the column marked *ideal*. Now go around the room and collect information from your classmates about the ages at which these activities are permitted in the countries that they know about. Do not forget to include information about this country as well.

Activity	Ideal Age	Real Age/Countries					
drive a car							
drink alcohol							
vote							
join the military							
get married							
own a gun							
buy cigarettes							

When you have collected the information, prepare a report (oral or written) on the differences and similarities you found across different countries. Include your own opinions about the ideal ages for these activities and give reasons to support them. Remember to announce the purpose of the report in your introduction and to end with a concluding statement. You can use these headings to organize your information:

Introduction: Purpose of this report:

Most interesting similarities among countries:

Most interesting differences among countries:

Your opinions on ideal ages, with reasons to support them:

Brief concluding statement:

If you make a written report, remember to read it through carefully after you finish writing. Check to see if you were able to include any of the language discussed in this unit.

If you make an oral report, try to record your presentation and listen to it later. See if you were able to include any of the language discussed in this unit.

Activity 3

The purpose of this activity is to share opinions on different social issues. Work with a partner and look at the issues listed below. Relate the issues to this country and to other countries you know about. For each issue, think about sufficiency (enough–?), insufficiency (not enough—?), and excess (too —?), Try to be as specific as possible. Use the chart to record your ideas. We have offered some ideas to get you started, but you probably have better ideas of your own. Be ready to share your ideas with the rest of the class.

Issue	This Country	Other Countries
Public Transportation	—too expensive —not enough mass transit	Switzerland: very efficient
Health Care		
Housing		
Law and Order		
Employment		
Education		
Care of the Elderly		
Building and Public Transport Access For Disabled People		

Activity 4

Choose *one* of the social issues you discussed in Activity 3. Review the information you collected on different countries. In your opinion, which country has the best solution? Which country, in your opinion, is the least successful in dealing with this issue? Write a short report, describing the best and worst solutions. Give reasons to support your opinions. Remember to introduce your topic; we have suggested one possibility below, but you can probably think of a better way. When you finish writing, read your report carefully and check to see if you were able to include any of the language discussed in this unit.

In the modern world, many countries are trying to find solutions to the same social issues, and

it is interesting to see that different countries and cultures deal with these issues in different ways.

In my opinion, some countries have better solutions than others. To illustrate this point, I will talk

about _____ (social issue) _____ and show how _____

(country) _____ and _____ (country) _____ both deal

with it.

Activity 5

What is your ideal house or apartment like? Draw a plan of the house or apartment you would really like to live in. Next, write a short description of the house or apartment in which you are living at the moment, showing how it differs from your ideal house or apartment.

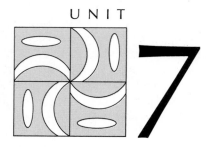

7

Giving Opinions and Advice

Should, Ought To, Had Better, Could, and Must

Task
Men's Work, Women's Work?

Look at the occupations below. Who *usually* does these jobs, men (♂), women (♀), or both (♂♀)? In your opinion, who is best suited to doing these jobs, men, women, or both? Write ♂, ♀, or ♂♀ in the appropriate column on the chart. Share your opinions with a partner.

Job	Who Usually Does It?		Who Should Do It?	
	in the U.S.	in your country	in the U.S.	in your country
elementary school teacher				
fire fighter				
airline pilot				
secretary				
cleric				
plumber				
nurse				
baby-sitter				
electrician				
fighter pilot				
cab driver				
college professor				

Focus 1

MEANING

Expressing Opinions and Beliefs

MEANING

- To show you think something is a good idea or that it is right for people to do, you can use *should* or *ought to:*

    (a) In my opinion, more men $\begin{Bmatrix} \textbf{should} \\ \textbf{ought to} \end{Bmatrix}$ teach in elementary schools.

- To show something is a bad idea or that it is not right for people to do, you can use *should not (shouldn't):*

    (b) In Alonso's opinion, women **should not** drive cabs.

Focus 2

FORM

Should and *Ought To*

FORM

- *Should* and *ought to* are modal auxiliaries. They do not take *s* in the third person singular:

    (a) She **should** be a doctor.

    (b) He **ought to** work with children.

- Questions and negatives are made without *do:*

    (c) **Should** we go? No, you **shouldn't.**

- *Ought to* is rarely used in questions and negatives.
- It is important to remember that *should* does not take *to*.

Exercise 1

Get together with another student. Choose four of the occupations from the chart and write down your partner's opinions on who is best suited (or not) to do them. Also show why she or he thinks this. (Information from Unit 6 may help you with this part.)

1. In _____ 's opinion, _____ (should/should not)

   _____ because _____

   _____.

2. She or he also thinks that _____ ought to

   because _____.

3. In addition, she or he believes that _____

   because _____.

4. Finally, _____

   _____.

Focus 3

USE

Advice and Opinions

USE

- *Should/should not* and *ought to/ought not to* express the speaker's opinion about a situation. Therefore, they are usually used when you need to give advice to somebody or when you want to give your opinion about a topic or situation.

Exercise 2

In the United States, many "self-help" books are published every year. These books give people advice on what they should do in order to improve their lives in specific ways. Look at the list of book titles and the extracts below. Match each extract to the book you think it probably comes from.

BOOK TITLES

How to Stay Married for a Long Time   Lose 30 Pounds in 30 Days
Caring for a Neurotic Cat   Live Longer, Eat Better
How to Dress For Success   How to Attract Women
Getting along with Your Coworkers   Ways to Save the Planet

EXTRACTS

1. You should try not to surprise him or her. Any kind of change should be introduced gradually and slowly. Take things slowly, and he or she will soon be happy to accept whatever you propose.

2. As an important first step, you really ought to eliminate red meat. This may be hard at first, but you will be amazed at how many healthy alternatives exist.

3. Honesty is not always the best policy. In some situations, you should not say exactly what you think; the truth might cause more trouble than it is worth. For example, you should try to be tactful and diplomatic when called upon to settle an argument, by trying to show that you value both points of view.

4. Learn to cook! You ought to learn some unusual and exotic dishes that you can prepare in advance. Pretend that it was easy and effortless to prepare so you can focus your attention on *her* and not on the meal. Wait for her to compliment you on your skill as a chef. Remember you should never beg for compliments!

5. Organize the people in your office! The office manager ought to arrange special bins for different types of paper, for bottles, and for cans. Make everybody at work feel they have a part to play.

6. You should never settle into a regular routine. Surprise each other with fun activities, like picnics after work or moonlight barbecues on the beach.

7. You should try to motivate yourself to keep going on. Buy a dress that is just a little bit too small and hang it in your closet. You should look at it every day and dream of the day when it will really fit you.

8. You should not draw attention to yourself. Choose conservative but becoming styles because you ought to look competent and professional at all times.

Exercise 3

Choose three of the book titles from Exercise 2 and write other appropriate pieces of advice. Use *should, ought to,* and *should not* as necessary.

Focus 4

Should versus *Must*

USE

- *Should* shows that something is a good idea:
  (a) A: I can't sleep at night.
  B: You **should** drink a glass of milk before you go to bed.
  B is giving advice, but *A* is not obliged to follow that advice. *A* is free to do what she or he pleases.

- *Must* is much stronger:
  (b) A: I don't have a driver's license.
  B: You **must** get a license before you drive.
  B is giving advice, but in this situation, it is obligatory for *A* to follow the advice. *A* is not free to do what she or he pleases.

- Refer to Unit 8 for more information on *must*.

Exercise 4

Oscar has just bought a used car. Complete the following, using *should, shouldn't, or must,* as appropriate. Different people may have different opinions about some of these, so be ready to justify your choices.

1. He _____ get insurance as soon as possible.

2. He _____ take it to a reliable mechanic and have it checked.

3. He _____ get registration.

4. He _____ drive it without insurance.

5. He _____ drink and drive.

6. He _____ wear a seat belt.

7. He _____ lock the doors when he parks the car.

8. He _____ keep a spare key in a safe place.

Focus 5

Should and *Ought To* versus *Had Better*

USE

- You can also use *had better* to give advice.

  Had better is much stronger than *should* and *ought to,* but not as strong as *must*:

  (a) You **should** go to school tomorrow. (I think it's a good idea for you to do this.)

  (b) You **had better** go to school tomorrow. (If you don't go, something bad will happen.)

  In this situation, *had better* suggests that there will be a negative result if you do not follow the advice.

  - *Had better* also expresses more urgency than *should:*

    (c) You **should** see a doctor about that. (It's a good idea.)

    (d) You **had better** see a doctor about that. (It's urgent.)

    (e) You **must** see a doctor about that. (It's obligatory.)

  - *Had better* is often used in situations in which the speaker has power or authority over the hearer:

    (f) Teacher to student: If you want to pass this class, you **had better** finish all your assignments.

    (g) Student to teacher: If you come to my country, you **should** visit Kyoto.

- In situations in which there is a power difference between speaker and hearer, *had better* sounds like an order or a command. Therefore, if you are not sure about the relationship between the speaker and the listener, it is always "safe" to use *should* or *ought to.*

Focus 6

Had Better

FORM

- *Had better* refers to the present and the future. It does not refer to the past, even though it is formed with *had:*
    - **(a)** You **had better** finish this tomorrow.
    - **(b)** I **had better** leave now.
    - **(c)** He **had better** pay me for this.
- *Had* is often contracted to *'d:*
    - **(d)** You**'d better** leave me alone.
- To form the negative, use *had better not:*
    - **(e)** You**'d better not** leave me alone.
    - **(f)** You **had better not** finish this late.

Exercise 5

Complete the following with *should, ought to, must,* or *had better* as necessary.

1. Inez:　　How can I register to take the TOEFL?

　　Patsy:　　First you ＿＿＿＿＿＿＿ complete this application form.

2. Naoko:　　I want to get a good score on the TOEFL, but I'm not sure how to do that.

　　Kate:　　I think you ＿＿＿＿＿＿＿ take every opportunity to practice your English.

3. Yu-shan:　　I'm sorry I haven't been coming to class recently.

　　Advisor:　　You ＿＿＿＿＿＿＿ start attending regularly if you want to stay in this

　　　　program.

4. Herbert:　　I think I'm getting the flu.

　　Eleanor:　　You ＿＿＿＿＿＿＿ go to bed and drink plenty of orange juice.

5. Claudia:　　I've lost my credit card.

　　Rafael:　　You ＿＿＿＿＿＿＿ report it immediately.

6. Doctor: You _____ take these pills four times a day.

7. Mother: Time for bed!

   Calvin: Just five more minutes.

   Mother: No! You _____ come here at once or else I won't read you a bed-

   time story.

8. Carmen: I'd love to visit Poland.

   Carol: Well, first of all, you _____ get a special visa.

9. Debbie: I've got a sore throat.

   James: You _____ try not to talk too much.

10. Lois: You _____ clean up your room immediately. If you don't, there

   will be trouble.

Exercise 6

Circle the *best* response in the following:

1. You (should not/must not) smoke when you are in a movie theater in the United States.
2. While you are in Los Angeles, you (had better/should) try to visit Disneyland.
3. In the state of Michigan, people under the age of 21 (should not/must not) purchase alcohol.
4. Children (should/had better) wear helmets when they ride bicycles.
5. Look, the bus is coming! We (should/had better) run if we want to catch it.
6. Everybody who comes into the United States (must/should) show a valid passport or I.D.
7. I've just spilled coffee on the new rug. I (should/had better) clean it up right away before it stains.
8. Professor Katz gets really angry when students chew gum in class. You (had better/should) get rid of your gum before we get to class.
9. Tourists visiting my hometown in the spring (had better/should) bring cameras, as it's very beautiful at that time of year.
10. My brother is looking for a new girlfriend. He (must/should) take cooking classes, and maybe he'll meet someone there.

Focus 7

Should versus *Could*

USE

- You can also use *could* to express opinions or to give advice. However, *could* is much weaker than *should* because it only expresses possible options or possibilities for action in a situation; it does not show that the speaker necessarily thinks this a good idea or that it is right:

  (a) You **should** see that movie. (I think it is a good idea for you to see it.)

  (b) You **could** see that movie. (It is possible for you to see that movie if you want to.)

- We often use *could* when we want to suggest all the possiblities that are available to somebody, without saying which one we think is best:

  (c) If you want to improve your Spanish, you **could** take classes, you **could** listen to Spanish-speaking stations on the radio, you **could** find a conversation partner, or you **could** take a vacation in Mexico.

Exercise 7

Look back at the occupations in the Task at the beginning of the unit. Are there any occupations that are usually done by men that you think are possible for women to do and vice versa? Write your answers below, using *could*. Share your ideas with the rest of the class.

Men could _____ , but usually they don't.

Women could _____ , but _____

_____

_____

_____

Can you think of any other occupations that men could do but usually do not? Can you think of any that women could do but usually don't?

Exercise 8

Look at the following situation and respond to the questions below.

A woman went shopping. First she bought a large piece of cheese. Then she stopped at a pet store to buy a white mouse for her nephew's birthday. Just as she was leaving the store, she saw an adorable black and white cat. She couldn't leave the store without it, so she bought the cat as well.

Unfortunately, her car is parked a long way from the pet store, and she can only carry one thing at a time. What could she do in order to get everything to her car? How many solutions can you find?

She could _____

_____

_____

_____

There are no parking areas near the pet store, so she cannot move her car, and there is nobody around to help her. Unfortunately, cats eat mice and mice eat cheese. This means that if she leaves the cat with the mouse, the cat will eat the mouse and if she leaves the mouse with the cheese, the mouse will eat the cheese.

What should she do? What is the best solution to her problem?

She should _____

_____

You can find the solution to this problem at the end of the unit.

Focus 8

USE

Should and *Ought To* versus *Could, Had Better,* and *Must*

USE

As you have seen, although all these modal auxiliaries express opinions and give advice, they express different degrees of strength:

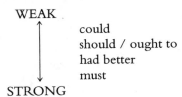

WEAK

could
should / ought to
had better
must

STRONG

Activities

Activity 1

Read the following situation and follow the instructions given:

Jennifer is an American student. She is planning to major in international business and has decided that it would be advantageous if she knew how to speak Japanese. Therefore, she borrowed some money from her father and went to Japan for six months. She has been in Tokyo for three months, taking classes in Japanese language and conversation. When she first arrived, she was overwhelmed by culture shock, so she quickly made friends with other Americans she met. Instead of living with a Japanese host family, she decided to move in with two other American women. Now she spends all her time with her new friends. She takes Japanese classes every day, but she talks only to the other English-speaking students and she seldom spends any time with the students who do not speak any English. As a result, she rarely speaks any Japanese and has not made much progress in the language; she has not learned much about Japanese culture either. She is having a lot of fun in Tokyo with her friends, but now she has a serious problem. Her father has just called to tell her that he will be coming to Tokyo on business, and he wants her to help him while he is there. He wants her to help interpret for him, and he also wants her to help advise him on the culture and customs. She is feeling very anxious about meeting her father.

First, brainstorm and write a list of all the *possible* solutions to Jennifer's problem that you can think of in two minutes. Then get together with two or three other students and share your solutions. Look at all the possibilities you can think of and then select from these the three *best*. Be ready to share these with the rest of the class and to justify them as necessary.

Activity 2

Get together with another student and choose one of the following topics. How many different ideas can you come up with?

    How to get a traffic ticket
    How to get rid of your boyfriend / girlfriend
    How to avoid learning English
    How to get an *F* in this class
    How to annoy your roommate

With your partner, make a poster presentation on the topic you chose. Take a large poster-sized sheet of paper or card and use it to make a poster that expresses your ideas. You can use graphics, pictures, and diagrams to make your poster informative and eye-catching. Display your poster and use it to explain your ideas to the rest of the class.

Activity 3

Many American newspapers have advice columns to which people write and for help with their problems. Three famous ones are "Dear Abby," "Ann Landers," "Miss Manners." Clip any advice columns you can find in various newspapers and bring them to class. Circulate the letters without their replies. In groups, try to come up with helpful advice. Share your responses with the rest of the class. Compare your advice with the advice the professionals gave.

Activity 4

In groups, write a letter to "Dear Abby," asking for advice on a particular problem. Exchange your problem letter with another group and write solutions to their problem. Share both problem and solution with the rest of the class.

Activity 5

Write a short report, giving advice to someone who is planning on visiting your hometown, your country, or the community where you grew up. Advise him or her on places to visit, clothes to wear, things to bring, things to do, and how to act. When you finish writing, check your report and see how you have used the language discussed in this unit. It is not necessary to use a modal auxiliary in every sentence, as this would sound very unnatural! Remember to start your report with an introductory statement. For example: my hometown/country, (name), is very interesting, and if you follow my advice, I am sure that you will have an enjoyable and rewarding visit. . . .

Activity 6

Read the following and circle *should* or *should not* to express the point of view that is closest to your own opinion on the topic.

1. School uniforms should/should not be obligatory.
2. Animals should/should not be used in laboratory experiments.
3. Doctors should/should not reveal the identity of AIDS patients.
4. Mothers should/should not work outside the home when their children are young.
5. A woman should/should not take her husband's family name when she marries.

Choose the topic that interests you the most and then go around the room until you find one or two other students who share your opinion on that topic. Form a group with these students and brainstorm all the reasons and examples you can think of to support your point of view and then write them down. Choose the strongest ones, with the best examples, and use them to make a short report (oral or written) presenting your opinion. Share your report with the rest of the class and be ready to justify your position as necessary.

Solution To The Problem In Exercise 8

This is a version of a well-known logic problem. First, the woman should take the mouse to the car, leaving the cat with the cheese. Next, she should return and pick up the cat and take it to the car. As soon as she gets to the car with the cat, she should remove the mouse and take it with her, leaving the cat in the car. When she gets back to the shopping area, she should pick up the cheese and leave the mouse. Then she should take the cheese to the car and leave it there with the cat. Finally, she should return to collect the mouse and bring it with her to the car.

There are many different versions of this problem. Do you know one? Share it with the rest of the class.

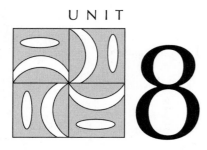

UNIT

8

Phrasal Modals and Modals of Necessity

Have To/Have Got To, Do Not Have To, Must/Must Not, Should

Task
Entering the United States

A friend of yours from Japan is planning a short trip to California. She is going to fly directly from Tokyo to San Francisco. She doesn't have room for too many things because she wants to take only a backpack with her. Here are some of the things she is thinking of taking.

a visa traveler's checks	
a camera a lot of clothes a gun	
a passport drugs skis	
a dictionary photographs of her hometown food	
an international driver's license 10 bottles of cognac	
a map of the U.S. books about her country a credit card	
fresh fruit	

Can you help her? Look at the categories below. With a partner, try to put all the things she wants to take in the appropriate categories.

#1 It's prohibited.	#2 It's OK, but it isn't necessary.	#3 It's a good idea.	#4 It's necessary and obligatory—you can't enter the U. S. without it.

Focus 1

Obligation, Necessity, and Prohibition

MEANING

- To show something is necessary and obligatory, you can say:
  - **(a)** You **must have** a passport.
    OR
  - **(b)** You **have to have** a passport.
    OR
  - **(c)** You **have got to have** a passport.
- To show something is a good idea, you can say:
  - **(d)** You **should bring** a camera.
- To show something is permitted but isn't necessary, you can say:
  - **(e)** You **don't have to bring** a lot of clothes.
- To show something is prohibited and absolutely not permitted, you can say:
  - **(f)** You **must not (mustn't) bring** drugs into the United States.

Exercise 1

Underline the sentences that have the same meaning.

1. **a.** When you visit India, you should have a visa.
   b. When you visit India, you have to have a visa.
   c. When you visit India, you must have a visa.

2. **a.** Chan wants to go to graduate school, so he has to get a good TOEFL score.
   b. Chan wants to go to graduate school, so he has got to get a good TOEFL score.
   c. Chan wants to go to graduate school, so he must get a good TOEFL score.

What differences can you see between the *forms* of 2a and 2c? Between 2b and 2c?

Focus 2

Modals and Phrasal Modals of Necessity

FORM

- *Must* is a modal and does not change in form to agree with the subject:

  (a) I **must** go now and he **must** go too.

- *Have to* and *have got to* are phrasal modals. They are different from modals because they contain more than one word and end in *to*. Phrasal modals change in form to agree with the subject:

  (b) I **have to** go now and he **has to** go too.

- Modals versus phrasal modals: statements

Modal *must*	Phrasal Modal *have to*	*have got to*
I must go. She must go.	I have to go. She has to go.	I have (I've) got to go. She has (She's) got to go.

- Modals versus phrasal modals: questions

Modal *must*	Phrasal Modal *have to*	*have got to*
Must I go? Must she go?	Do I have to go? Does she have to go?	Have I got to go? Has she got to go?

Exercise 2

What do the following road signs mean? What happens if you do not obey them? Make a statement for each sign that explains what you have to do when you are driving and you see this sign. The first one has been done for you as an example.

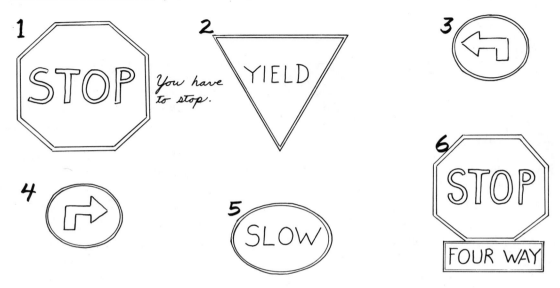

1. STOP — *You have to stop.*
2. YIELD
3. (left turn arrow)
4. (right turn arrow)
5. SLOW
6. STOP FOUR WAY

Focus 3

MEANING

Advice versus Necessity

MEANING

- Modals and phrasal modals have many different meanings. In exercise 2, you were expressing **necessity**: When drivers see a stop sign like the one in #1, it is **necessary** for them to stop or they will break the traffic law. As you saw in the Task, we can express necessity with the modal *must* or with the phrasal modals *have to* and *have got to*.

- The modal *should* is not as strong as *must, have to,* and *have got to*.

  - As you saw in the Task, *should* shows that something is a good idea and expresses advice but not necessity.

- For more information on the use of *should* to give advice and opinions, see Unit 7.

85

Exercise 3

Turn back to the Task. Find the things that are necessary for your friend to take. Write statements about them below.

NECESSARY

_____

_____

_____

Exercise 4

Decide which of the following are *necessary* to do if you want to get a driver's license in the United States.

speak English very well

know how to drive

practice before the test

take an eye test

take a written test

have a medical examination

own a car

pass a driving test

drive on the right

study the information booklet from the Department of Motor Vehicles (the department that issues driver's licenses)

Exercise 5

Your friend wants to know what he has to do to get a driver's license. Make statements to explain what it is necessary for him to do if he wants to get a driver's license in the United States; then explain what it is necessary for him to do if he wants to get a driver's license in your country.

Focus 4

Have To versus Have Got To

USE

- Generally, *have to* is more neutral than *have got to*. In other words, *have got to* is very strong; use this when you want to emphasize that you feel something is very important and very necessary:

  (a) Joe **has got to** follow a very strict diet because he has a serious heart condition.

Exercise 6

Make a statement for each situation below. For each one, decide which you would use, *have to* or *have got to*.

1. Your sister's four-year-old son takes a nap every day and goes to bed at 8:00 every night. But

   today he didn't take a nap, and it's now 10:00 P.M.

   She says to her son, "You _____ go to sleep now."

2. The last time your friend went to the dentist was four years ago. He doesn't think he has any

   problems with his teeth, but he feels he should probably go to the dentist for a checkup.

   He says, "I _____ make an appointment to see the dentist sometime soon."

3. You haven't been reading the assignments for your history class, and you did very badly on the

   first two quizzes. You are afraid that you'll fail the course.

   You tell your classmate, "I _____ study every day if I don't want to fail my

   history class."

4. Your roommate is making dinner. She has just put a loaf of bread in the oven. Suddenly she

   realizes that she doesn't have an important item that she needs for dessert.

   She says, "I _____ go to the store. If I'm not back in ten minutes, can you take

   the bread out of the oven? It _____ come out at 7:00."

Focus 5

MEANING

Expressing Prohibition:
Must Not / Mustn't

- When you want to show that something is not permitted or is prohibited, you can use *must not* or the contracted form *mustn't*:

  (a) You **mustn't** smoke in here.

- *Must not* and *mustn't* are often used as a strong command in situations where the speaker definitely wants the listener to obey:

  (b) You **must not** have any more!

Exercise 7

Look at the cartoon. Write statements using *must not* to describe each prohibited activity.

1. _____

2. _____

3. _____

4. _____

5. _____

6. _____

7. _____

8. _____

Exercise 8

Look at the photos. With a partner, try to figure out what the signs mean in each one. What is the difference between the two photographs? Work with your partner and try to complete the summary below.

PHOTOGRAPH A

PHOTOGRAPH B

DO YOU NEED CHANGE
FOR THE
BUS
TELEPHONE, WASHING MACHINE, ETC.

WE GIVE CHANGE WITH A SMILE
NO PURCHASE NECESSARY

Reprinted with permission from Mark Chester, *No in America*, Taylor Publishing Co, Dallas (1986).

In Photograph A, you _____,

but in Photograph B, you _____.

Focus 6

Necessity, No Necessity, and Prohibition

- **Must, have to,** and **have got to** versus **do not have to:**
  - *Must, have to,* and *have got to* show that it is necessary to do something:
    - **(a)** If you want change, you **must** buy something.
    - **(b)** If you want change, you **have to** buy something.
    - **(c)** If you want change, you **have got to** buy something.
  - *Do not have to* shows that it is not necessary to do something:
    - **(d)** If you want change, you **don't have to** buy anything.
- **Must not** versus **do not have to:**
  - *You must do it* and *You have to do it* have the same meaning:
    - **(e)** You **have to** have a valid passport to travel overseas.
    - **(f)** You **must** have a valid passport to travel overseas.
  - However, *You must not do it* and *You do not have to do it* do NOT have the same meaning.
  - *You do not have to do it* means it is not necessary for you to do it:
    - **(g)** There aren't any classes on Saturday, so you **don't have to** come to school.
  - *You must not do it* means it is prohibited:
    - **(h)** You **mustn't** smoke in the movie theater.

Exercise 9

Turn back to the Task. Find three things that are prohibited and three things that (in your opinion) are not necessary. Write statements about them below.

PROHIBITED

1. _____ .

2. _____ .

3. _____ .

NOT NECESSARY

1. _____ .

2. _____ .

3. _____ .

Exercise 10

Turn back to Exercise 4. Find three things that are not necessary to do to get a driver's license and write statements about them below.

1. _____ .

2. _____ .

3. _____ .

Exercise 11

Peter is an athlete. Every week his coach gives him a different training schedule. Read his current schedule and complete the sentences below, using *have to, do not have to,* and *must not.*

TRAINING SCHEDULE					
	M	**T**	**W**	**T**	**F**
Necessary	lift weights	run 15 miles	cycle 50 miles	rest and eat high–calorie food	run 20 miles
Not Necessary	run	swim	lift weights	take a sauna	cycle
Prohibited	drink coffee	eat meat	eat dairy products	exercise	drink milk

1. Peter has to _____ on Monday.

2. He doesn't have to _____ .

3. He must not _____ .

4. _____ . (drink milk)

5. _____ . (swim)

6. _____ . (run 20 miles)

7. _____ . (rest/ take a sauna)

Now make your own sentences about Peter's training schedule. Do not use information from sentences 1–7.

8. _____ .

9. _____ .

10. _____ .

Focus 7

FORM

Talking about the Past:
Have To and *Must*

FORM

- "He **has to** exercise every day, but he **doesn't have to** swim" refers to regular habits, so you use the present.
- To talk about the past, change *have* and *has* to *had:*
  He had to exercise last week, but he **didn't have to swim.**
- There is no past tense form of *must* when it is used to express necessity. When you want to express necessity in the past, use *have to*. Do not use *must* to talk about past necessity:

Present	Past
We **have to** go. We **must** go.	We **had to** go.

Exercise 12

Maggie is telling her friend Jan about a terrible job she had last year. Complete their conversation with *must, have to,* and *do not have to* in the present or in the past, as appropriate.

Maggie: My worst job was when I worked as a waitress last summer.

Jan: What was so terrible about it?

Maggie: First, I (1) _____ get up at 5:00 A.M.

Jan: Did you drive to work?

Maggie: No. I didn't have a car then, so I (2) _____ walk two miles.

Jan: What time (3) _____ be at the restaurant?

Maggie: 6:00.

Jan: 6:00. How awful! Did you wear a uniform?

Maggie: No, we (4) _____ wear a special uniform or anything, but the work was really hard.

Jan: What about your present job?

Maggie: Oh, I *love* my present job. You see, I start work at 11:00 A.M., so I (5) _____ get up early, and the people are really nice.

Jan: (6) _____ work on weekends?

Maggie: No, I (7) _____ work on weekends, but that's not so good.

Jan: Why?

Maggie: My boyfriend (8) _____ work on weekends, so I never see him.

Jan: That's no problem—find a new boyfriend!

Focus 8

Talking about the Future: *Must* and *Have To*

FORM

- To talk about necessity in the future, use *will (not)* before *have to*:
  - **(a)** **We will (we'll) have to** repaint the house in a couple of years.
  - **(b)** **We will not (won't) have to** paint the house again for a couple of years.
- You can also use *must* to talk about future necessity or prohibition:
  - **(c)** We **must** go to the bank tomorrow.
  - **(d)** You **must not / mustn't** park here tomorrow.
- Do NOT use *will* with *must*:
  - **(e)** I **must** call him next week,
    NOT: I will must call him next week.

Exercise 13

Complete the following, using *will have to* and *won't have to* in the appropriate places.

Some people are pessimistic about life in the future because it will be necessary to do many different things. They think that we (1) _____ (change) our habits. For example, to protect the environment, we (2) _____ (develop) materials that do not cause pollution. In addition, we (3) _____ (drive) less, and we (4) _____ (try) to develop different methods of transportation. If we continue to use the automobile as much as we do today, in the future we (5) _____ (wear) oxygen masks to protect us from the polluted air.

However, other people are optimistic about the future because they think it won't be necessary to do many of the things we have to do today. For example, we (6) _____ (leave) home to shop because we will buy everything by computer. Furthermore, we (7) _____ (work) every day and also, we (8) _____ (cook) because we will use pills instead of food.

Can you add ideas of your own about things we will have to do in the future and things we will not have to do? Share your ideas with the rest of the class.

Exercise 14

Read the conversations below carefully and complete the missing parts.

CONVERSATION A

Ann has just finished talking on the phone with Tom. When she hangs up the phone, her friend Bill wants to know about their conversation.

Bill: You sound worried. Is Tom having problems?

Ann: Tom's landlord sold the apartment house, so Tom (1) _____ find another place to live.

Bill: Oh, that's too bad. When (2) _____ (he) move out of his apartment?

Ann: I think he (3) _____ move out by the end of the month.

CONVERSATION B

Emily, a five-year-old, is playing in the street. Her mother, who is watching from the house, suddenly runs out to her. A big car zooms by.

Emily's mother: Emily! You (4) _____ be more careful! Don't cross the street

without looking for cars!

Emily: But I didn't see the car!

Emily's mother: You (5) _____ look in both directions before you cross the street.

CONVERSATION C

Outside the classroom, you hear a conversation between your teacher and Wang, one of your classmates.

Your teacher: Wang, I'm afraid this is the last time I'm going to tell you this. You

(6) _____ hand in your homework on time.

Wang: I know, I know. But—

Your teacher: No more excuses! You really (7) _____ try to keep up with the class

if you want to pass.

CONVERSATION D

It's the end of the school year. Ron and Marion have just had their last class of the term.

Ron: It's vacation time at last! We (8) _____ work for two months!

Marion: Not me. My grades were very bad, so I (9) _____ study all through the

summer.

Ron: I know how that feels. I failed physics two years ago, and I (10) _____

read physics books all summer—and my friends just went to the beach every day. They

(11) _____ study at all.

Activities

Activity 1

In Exercise 8, you saw some examples of signs. The purpose of this activity is to create signs of your own and have your classmates guess what they mean. Come up with some ideas for "prohibited" signs. Here are some possibilities, but there are many more:

You mustn't feed the ducks.   You mustn't eat in class.
You mustn't sleep in class.   You mustn't drink this water.

When you have thought of something, draw a sign to represent it. Do not write the command next to the sign—your classmates must guess what it is. Look at their signs and write down what you think they mean.

Activity 2

In this activity, you will be comparing your childhood memories with your classmates'. Think back to when you were a child. Think of five things you had to do then that you do not have to do now. Then think of five things you did not have to do then that you have to do now. Next, compare your list with those of two or three other classmates and be ready to report on your findings to the rest of the class.

You		Your Classmates	
Childhood	**Now**	**Childhood**	**Now**

Activity 3

What about children in this country today? Do they have to do things that you did not have to do? Are there any things that children in this country today do not have to do?

Use the lists you and your partners made and interview two or three different children (or parents of children) to find out if they have to or do not have to do these things too. Write a report on your findings, entitled, "Children's Lives: Past and Present." Make sure that your report has a brief introduction and that all your ideas relate to the topic. When you finish, read your report carefully and check to see how you have used the language practiced in this unit.

Activity 4

Do you know how to get a driver's license in any other countries in the world? What do you have to do to get a license there? In what ways is it different here? Talk to your classmates and find out what they know. Be ready to report on your findings.

Activity 5

Do you know what a person has to do in order to get any of the following?

a green card (for permanent residence in the United States)
a Social Security number
a marriage license
a license for a gun

Choose *one* and find out as much information as you can. If possible, ask a native speaker to tell you what he or she knows about the topic and record his or her answers. Be ready to share your information with the rest of the class.

Activity 6

A friend of yours is interested in studying at a North American university. Write him/her a letter, explaining what he or she will have to do in order to enter a university.

Expressing Likes and Dislikes

Rejoinder Phrases, Hedges, Gerunds as Subjects and Objects

Task

In this task, you will be exchanging opinions about different kinds of food and comparing your findings.

Work with a partner. One of you is *A,* the other is *B*. Complete the chart together. In the top left-hand box, write three kinds of food that *A* likes and *B* likes too. Next, in the top right-hand box, write three kinds of food that *A* does not like, but *B* does. After that, in the bottom left-hand corner, write three kinds of food *B* doesn't like, but *A* does. Finally, in the last box, write three kinds of food that *A* does not like and *B* does not either.

		A	
		I like	**I don't like**
B	**I like**	(*A* likes and *B* likes too.)	(*A* doesn't like, but B does.)
	I don't like	(*B* doesn't like, but *A* does.)	(*B* doesn't like and *A* doesn't either.)

Focus 1

Expressing Similarity

FORM
MEANING

- **Affirmative sentences:**
  - These sentences express similarity:
    - **(a)** I like fruit. Roberta likes fruit.
    - **(b)** I like fruit and Roberta does too.

    In each example, the subjects are different (*Roberta* and *I*), but everything else expresses similarity between us.
  - To form:
    - **(c)** I like fruit. Roberta likes fruit. → I like fruit **and** Roberta **does too.**
- **Negative sentences:**
  - **(d)** I don't eat meat. Roberta doesn't eat meat.
  - **(e)** I don't eat meat and Roberta doesn't either.
  - To form:
    - **(f)** I don't eat meat. Roberta doesn't eat meat. → I don't eat meat, **and** Roberta **doesn't either.**
  - Be careful with subject / verb agreement:
    - **(g)** NOT: I like chocolate and Roberta **do** too.
    - **(h)** NOT: I don't like hot dogs and Roberta **don't** either.

Exercise 1

Turn back to the information you shared in the Task. Write sentences using *too* and *either* as appropriate.

Focus 2

Expressing Similarity: Inverted Forms

FORM
MEANING

- **Affirmative sentences:**
  - **(a)** I like dancing and David **does** too.
  - **(b)** I like dancing and so **does** David.
    NOT: and so David does.

  These sentences all have the same meaning.

  - **(c)** I like dancing and so **do** David and Rena.
    NOT: and so David and Rena do.

- **Negative sentences:**
  - **(d)** I don't like country music and Bruce **doesn't** either.
  - **(e)** I don't like country music and neither **does** Bruce.
    NOT: and neither Bruce does.

  These sentences all have the same meaning.

  - **(f)** I don't like country music and neither **do** Gary and Bruce.
    NOT: and neither Gary and Bruce do.

  Neither is a negative word; therefore, do not use *not* with the second verb.

Exercise 2

Use the information you shared in the Task to write sentences using *so* and *neither*.

Exercise 3

Now work with a different partner and share the information on your charts in the Task. Use this information to complete the following report. Make sure that your statements are not only grammatical but also true.

My classmates and I have strong opinions about the kinds of food we like and dislike. For example,

_____ and so _____ .

_____ and neither _____ .

_____ too.

_____ either.

We also found other similarities in our taste in food. _____

either. _____ neither _____ .

_____ so _____ .

_____ too.

Focus 3

FORM

Expressing Similarity

FORM

When the verbs are the same but the subjects are different, do not repeat the second verb; instead, do one of the following:

• Use *do:*
   (a) I speak French and so **does** my mother.
      OR
• Use an auxiliary verb if the first verb is an auxiliary verb:
   (b) I **can** speak French and so **can** she.
   (c) I **have** seen it and so **have** you.
      OR
• Use *be* if the first verb is *be:*
   (d) I **am** happy and so **is** he.
   The second verb takes the same tense as the first verb.

Exercise 4

Match the first half of the sentences in Column A with the second half in Column B. Draw an arrow to show the connection. The first one has been done for you.

She is late	and so have I.
We saw it last night	and Peter didn't either.
They've never eaten there	and my brother can't either.
She'll call you tomorrow	and so is her boyfriend.
Barbara was looking sad	and we do too.
The children have seen that movie	and her friend was too.
You didn't do the right thing	and so will I.
I can't play tennis	and neither do we.
Her bike wasn't cheap	and we haven't either.
Scott doesn't have any money	and they did too.
The secretary speaks Spanish	and neither was her car.

Focus 4

USE

Rejoinder Phrases

USE

- Rejoinder phrases (*so do I, neither do I, I do too, I don't either*) are very common in conversation. We use them when we want to show agreement with somebody else's opinions or ideas:

  (a) Tina: I love going to the movies.
      Rob: **So do I.**

  (b) Tina: I never go to violent movies.
      Rob: **Neither do I.**

  (c) Tina: I don't like watching violence.
      Rob: **I don't either.**

  (d) Tina: I prefer comedies.
      Rob: Really? **I do too.**

- *Neither do I* and *so do I* emphasize the speaker's feelings about the topic.
  I do too and *I don't either* are more neutral because they do not emphasize the speaker's feelings as strongly.

Exercise 5

Read the comic strip. Can you find the missing parts of the conversation in the list below? Write the numbers in the appropriate cartoon bubble.

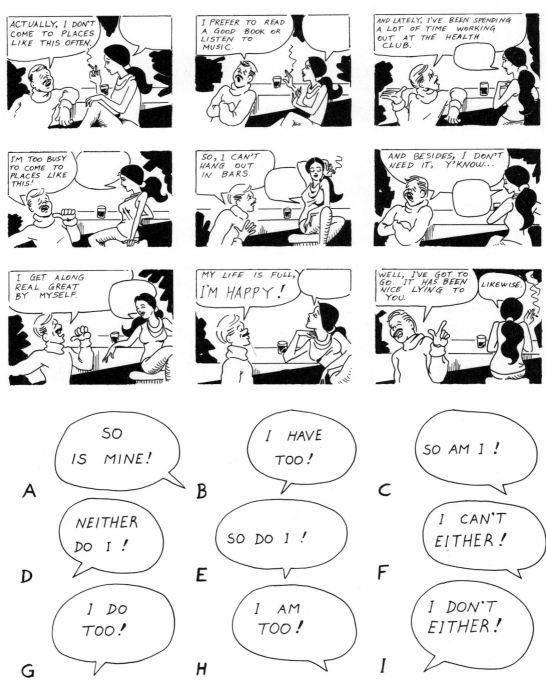

Focus 5

Hedges

USE

- In conversation, rejoinder phrases show agreement with the speaker:
  - **(a)** Stacey: I love ballet.
    - Jeff: **So do I!**
- However, if you do not agree strongly with the speaker's opinion, you can use a hedge:
  - **(b)** Stacey: I love ballet. What about you?
    - Jeff: **Sort of.**
  - **(c)** Stacey: Do you like opera?
    - Jeff: **Kind of.**

    Jeff does not like opera or ballet very much.
- *Sort of* and *kind of* are used in informal conversation. In fast speech, they are often reduced to *kinda* and *sorta*.
- Rejoinder phrases follow a statement:
  - **(d)** Stacey: I like basketball.
    - Jeff: **I do too.** OR **So do I.**
  - **(e)** Stacey: I don't like football.
    - Jeff: **I don't either.** OR **Neither do I.**
- Hedges often follow a question:
  - **(f)** Stacey: Do you like soccer?
    - Jeff: **Kind of.** OR **Sort of.**

Exercise 6

Claire and Chris have just met at a party and are finding out how much they have in common.

Look at the chart showing their likes and dislikes and complete the conversation below, using appropriate information from the chart. The first one has been done for you.

✔✔ = A LOT ✔ = A LITTLE

	Likes		Dislikes
CHRIS	swimming✔✔	hiking✔✔	TV✔✔
	cats✔✔	music✔	getting up in the morning✔✔
	cooking✔✔	Chinese food✔✔	rap music✔✔
CLAIRE	cats✔	cooking✔	rap music✔✔
	eating in✔✔	music✔✔	getting out of bed✔✔
	restaurants	swimming✔✔	staying home✔✔
	Chinese food✔✔	hiking✔	watching TV✔✔

Chris: Well, let me see ... what are some of my favorite things? The ocean ... I love swimming in the ocean.

Claire: (1) So do I. Maybe we should go for a swim sometime.

Chris: Yes, that'd be great! Do you like hiking too?

Claire: (2) _____ . In general, I prefer to be active. I mean, I don't like sitting home and watching TV.

Chris: (3) _____ . But I don't like getting up in the morning.

Claire: Well, (4) _____ . Most people don't like getting out of bed in the morning! What about music? Do you like music?

Chris: (5) _____ . I don't know too much about it, actually.

Claire: Really? I love all kinds of music, except for rap. I hate rap!

Chris: (6) _____ . We certainly agree on that one! What else? I love cooking; do you?

Claire: (7) _____ . I really prefer eating out in restaurants, especially in Chinatown. I really love Chinese food.

Chris: (8) _____ . I've heard that the new Chinese restaurant on Grant Avenue is supposed to be really good.

Claire: (9) _____ . Why don't we give it a try?

Chris: That sounds good. By the way, I have six cats. Do you like cats?

Claire: Well, (10) _____ .

Chris: That's OK—as long as you don't *hate* them. . . .

Exercise 7

One way to meet people is through personal ads in newspapers or magazines. These personal ads appeared in a local newspaper. Read them quickly and then read the statements that follow. Circle *T* (true) if you think the statement is true and *F* (false) is you think it is false.

(A) COULD THIS BE YOU?

You are attractive, slim, and athletic. You like dancing, eating candlelit dinners, and walking on the beach by moonlight. Like me, you also enjoy camping and hiking. You love dogs and you don't smoke. If you are the woman of my dreams, send a photo to Box 3092.

(C) I'VE GOT YOU ON MY WAVELENGTH

Athletic, professional, DF-animal lover seeks active man who knows how to treat a lady. Box 4021.

(B) BEAUTY & BRAINS

Warm, humorous, well-educated SWF loves walking on the beach, dancing, cycling, and hiking. Seeks intelligent life partner with compatible interests. PS - I'm allergic to cats, dogs, and smokers. Box 875.

(D) A FEW OF MY FAVORITE THINGS:

Cooking for my friends; cycling; walking on the beach with my dog; wise and witty women.
I can't stand: snobs; cheap wine; jogging; people who smoke; women who wear makeup.
DM looking for a special woman. Box 49

1. *A* likes walking on the beach and so do *D* and *B*. T F
2. *B* does not like smokers and neither do *A* and *C*. T F
3. Cooking for friends is one of *B's* favorite pastimes. T F
4. *D* does not like women who wear makeup. T F
5. *D* likes dancing, and *A* does too. T F
6. *A* wants to find someone who likes hiking, and so does *D*. T F
7. Jogging and cycling are two of *B*'s favorite sports. T F

Do you think any of these people would make a good couple? If so, why? If not, why not?

Focus 6

Gerunds as Subjects and Objects

FORM

- *Smoking, drinking,* and *dancing* are often used as **verbs**; however, you can also use them as **nouns**.
    - **(a)** He is **smoking** a cigarette right now. (part of a verb phrase)
    - **(b)** **Smoking** is bad for your health. (noun: subject of a sentence)
    - **(c)** Brian stopped **smoking** last month. (noun: object of a sentence)
- Gerunds are formed from verbs: **verb + -ing**: *Reading.* Gerunds work like nouns; therefore, they can be
    - **(d)** the **subject** of a sentence: **Cooking** is his favorite hobby.
    - **(e)** the **object** of a verb: He likes **cooking**.
    - **(f)** the **object** of a preposition: He talked about **cooking**.
    - **(g)** the **complement** of a sentence: His favorite hobby is **cooking**.

Exercise 8

1. Underline all the gerunds in Exercise 7.
2. Underline (with a broken line) all the gerunds that are subjects and circle the gerunds that are objects / complements in sentences 1, 3, 5, 6, and 7.

Activities

Activity 1

THINGS IN COMMON

The purpose of this activity is to share information with one other person and then to report to the rest of the class on what you find. In sharing information with your partner, try to find out *how many things you have in common*. Some ideas for starting your conversation are given below. When you have nothing more to say on this topic, decide on another one and find out what you have in common connected to that. Use the chart for your notes.

Topic	Notes
family	some ideas . . . brothers and sisters?/ grandparents alive?/father older than mother?

Activity 2

Form teams. Your job as a team is to find as many similarities as possible among the pairs of things listed below. The team that finds the most similarities is the winner.

1. an apple and an orange
2. learning a foreign language and learning to ride a bike
3. tennis and golf
4. hiking and jogging

Activity 3

Form pairs or groups of three.

1. Think of 15–20 statements using *so / too/ either/ neither*. Make sure they are meaningful. Write each statement on two cards, like this:

A	B
My parents live in Paris	and so does my sister
I don't like broccoli	and they don't either

   Therefore, if you have 20 statements, you will have 40 cards.

2. Get together with another pair or threesome.

3. Place all the *A* cards in one pile and all the *B* cards in another pile. Shuffle each deck of cards carefully.

4. Put the *A* pile facedown on the table.

5. Distribute the *B* cards among the players. Do not look at the cards and place them facedown on the table in front of you.

6. The first player turns over the first card from the *A* pile on the table and puts the first card from his or her *B* pile beside it. The player must not look at his or her card before putting it down on the table. The object of the game is to create meaningful sentences. If the two cards on the table do not make a meaningful match, the next player puts his or her *B* card down. The game continues in this way until a meaningful match is created. The first player to spot a match shouts "Match" to stop the game. If the match is acceptable, he or she collects all the *B* cards on the table. The next *A* card is then turned over and the game continues.

7. The player with the most cards at the end is the winner.
   This game should be played as quickly as possible.

Activity 4

Make a survey similar to the one in the Task and find out more about your classmates' likes and dislikes. You can ask about movies / movie stars / types of music / singers / musicians / sports, and so on. Make a report on your findings.

> Recently I made a survey of my classmates' likes and dislikes. I asked them their opinions on several different topics and would now like to share some of my findings with you. . . .

Activity 5

Write a personal ad for yourself like the ones in Exercise 7. Display the ads that the class writes and try to guess who wrote each ad.

Want and *Need*

Reprinted with permission of Chronicle Features, San Francisco

Task

You are shipwrecked on a desert island. Complete the list below.

Things I Need (because they are necessary for survival on the island)

1. _____
2. _____
3. _____
4. _____
5. _____
6. _____

Things I Want (because they will make me happy on the island)

1. _____
2. _____
3. _____
4. _____
5. _____
6. _____

Get together with a partner and compare your lists. Together make a new list, reflecting *both* your ideas.

1. _____   1. _____

2. _____   2. _____

3. _____   3. _____

4. _____   4. _____

Focus 1

MEANING

Want versus *Need*

MEANING

- *Want* expresses desires, things that would be nice to have, things that would make your life happier or more comfortable. (Unfortunately, we can sometimes only dream about the things we want in life!)
- *Need* is used for something that is necessary and essential.

Focus 2

FORM

Forming Statements with *Want* and *Need*

 FORM

- *Want* and *need* are followed by a noun or a noun phrase:
    - **(a)** I **want** a radio.
    - **(b)** Anthony **needs** some medicine.
    - **(c)** We **want** several good books.
    - **(d)** Carole **needed** a cup of coffee.
- *Want* and *need* are also followed by an infinitive:
    - **(e)** Jack **needed** to sleep.
    - **(f)** Delphine **wanted** to go.
    - **(g)** They **need** to eat more vegetables.
    - **(h)** We **want** to build a house.

Exercise 1

Share your final list from the Task with the rest of the class, using *want* and *need* as appropriate. (We want . . . /We need. . . .) Be ready to justify your choices.

Exercise 2

It is your birthday. Your family wants to buy you things that you really need. Make a list of three things that you really *need* right now. Beside each item, write a short description of the kind or type you really *want*. (You can specify color, make, size, material, etc.)

EXAMPLES: I *need* some warm clothes for winter.

I *want* a black leather jacket and a pair of dark brown boots.

WHAT I NEED	THE TYPE I WANT
1. _____	1. _____
2. _____	2. _____
3. _____	3. _____

Exercise 3

Look at the statements and decide what the person needs or wants, as appropriate. The items in the list at the end will help you, but you probably have better ideas of your own.

1. Help!!! I just cut my finger!

   She needs a Band-Aid.

2. I'm going to Hawaii next week, and I really don't like any of my summer clothes.

   She _____ .

3. I have a terrible toothache.

   You _____ .

4. I can't pick this pan up. It's too hot.

   He _____ .

5. Ugh! This grapefruit is too sour.

   I _____ .

6. This class is very boring!

   The students _____ .

7. I can't read the instructions on this bottle because the print is too small.

   He _____ .

8. No, thanks, I don't like red wine. Do you have anything else?

   He _____ .

9. Oh, no! The button has just come off my blouse, and I don't have time to fix it.

   She _____ .

10. Oh, no! The flowers are dying!

    They _____ .

a pot holder	a Band-Aid	new eyeglasses
a safety pin	a pair of binoculars	some new clothes
some salt	change classes	a needle and thread
some sugar	go to the dentist	some water
something to drink		

Focus 3

FORM

Negative Statements

FORM

- For negative statements, add
  - *do not (don't)* or *does not (doesn't)*:
    - **(a)** I **don't** want to go.
    - **(b)** They **do not** need to tell her.
    - **(c)** She **doesn't** want to drive.
  - *did not (didn't)*:
    - **(d)** We **didn't** need your help.
    - **(e)** He **didn't** want to see us.
- In negative statements with plural count nouns or with non-count nouns, *some* changes to *any*:
  - **(f)** They **need some** new books.
  - **(g)** They **don't need any** new books.
  - **(h)** She **wants some** sugar in her coffee.
  - **(i)** She **doesn't want any** sugar in her coffee.

Exercise 4

Estella is having a garage sale. These are some of the things she is selling. With other students, discuss whether or not you need or want any of these things.

picture frames	garden furniture	kitty litter
sofa cushions	rugs	candles
dishes	a bed	baby clothes
laundry soap	computer software	a washer and dryer
garden tools	computer paper	bath towels
fertilizer for houseplants	a stereo	old magazines

Exercise 5

Alessandro is going to cook dinner. The recipe requires:

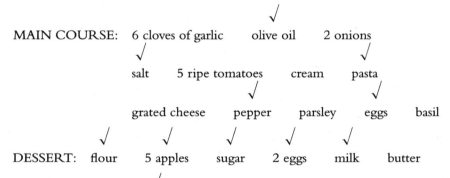

MAIN COURSE: 6 cloves of garlic ✓   olive oil ✓   2 onions

salt ✓   5 ripe tomatoes   cream   pasta ✓

grated cheese   pepper ✓   parsley   eggs ✓   basil

DESSERT: flour ✓   5 apples ✓   sugar ✓   2 eggs ✓   milk ✓   butter

Alessandro has checked (✓) the items he has already got in his kitchen. What does and doesn't he need to buy before he can start cooking?

Exercise 6

Use *want* or *need* to describe each situation below.

1. Peter realizes that it is necessary for him to borrow $100 to pay the rent this month.
2. Dan has a toothache. Suddenly he remembers that he has not been to a dentist in five years.
3. Hannah told her parents all the things she would like for her birthday next month: a doll, a bicycle, a teddy bear, and a cat.
4. Francisco is in class. He is bored, he does not like the teacher, and he does not like his classmates. He misses his girlfriend, who lives in Acapulco. Unfortunately, he is a long way from Acapulco.
5. I asked Ben if he wanted to buy some of my computer paper, but he had already bought some.
6. Mary offers her friend Karl some more wine, but he says he has a headache, and wine is bad for a headache.

Activities

Activity 1

Choose *one* of the following and with a partner, make a list of what you need to do in order to achieve it. Do other people agree with you?

1. get an *A* in this class
2. speak English fluently
3. become a citizen
4. keep in touch with old friends
5. get in better physical shape

Activity 2

"You Can't Always Get What You Want" is the the title of a Rolling Stones song. Interview different people outside the classroom to see how many people know the song and if they can remember any of the lyrics. Write down any words they can remember. Compare your findings with your classmates. If possible, try to get hold of the song and see if you can follow the words. What do you think the song means?

Activity 3

WHAT DO MEN AND WOMEN WANT?

If possible, divide into groups of the same sex (women work with women and men work with men). In your group, make a list of the characteristics you think are most important in your ideal partner. What things do you need and what things do you want?

What We Need	What We Want

Compare lists. Do men and women want and need the same things? Why or why not?

Activity 4

Some people who study literature believe that every character in every story has a clear motivation: They *want* or *need* something. To see if you agree with this, think of a short story or folktale or a movie that you know. Summarize the story and then, if you can, say what the main characters need or want.

Present Perfect

Since and *For*

Task

Quickly read the following:

MEDICAL HISTORY

NAME: Michael James Harris

MARITAL STATUS: Single

SERIOUS ILLNESS(ES):   None

SMOKING: Stopped 10 years ago

EYESIGHT: Wears glasses for reading; started in 1987

PRESENT PROBLEM: Headaches

SEX: Male   DATE OF BIRTH: 5/13/56

HEIGHT: 5 ft 11 in   WEIGHT: 185 lbs

TIME IN HOSPITAL: May 1973. Broke both legs in traffic accident

DRINKING: 1 glass of wine with dinner

ALLERGIES: None

WHEN PROBLEM STARTED: 2 months ago

Work with a partner and find details from Michael Harris's medical history to complete the following list. Find two things that relate to the past, two things that relate to the present, and two things that started in the past and continue to the present. The first one has been done for you.

PAST

1. *He broke his legs.*

2. _____

PRESENT

1. _____

2. _____

FROM PAST TO PRESENT

1. _____

2. _____

Focus 1

Present Perfect: Connecting Past and Present

 USE

- We use the present perfect to show a connection between something in the past and something in the present. The present perfect shows the result or relevance now of a past action, event, or experience.

PAST	PRESENT
February:	September:
(a) I **moved** to New York. (simple past)	**(b)** I **live** in New York now. (simple present)

FROM PAST TO PRESENT
(c) I **have lived** in New York since Febuary.
(d) I **have lived** in New York for seven months. (present perfect)

- In this situation, the simple past tells us only about the past; the present tells us only about the present. One use of the present perfect is to tell us about **something which began in the past and continues to the present**. For information about a different use of the present perfect, see Unit 12.

Focus 2

FORM

Forming the Present Perfect

 FORM

- *have/has* + past participle *

Statement	Negative	Question
I You We They } **have gone.** ('ve)	I You We They } **have not gone.** (**haven't**)	**Have** { I you we they } **gone?**
She He It } **has gone.** ('s)	She He It } **has not gone.** (**hasn't**)	**Has** { she he it } **gone?**

*See Appendix 1 on page 324 for the past participles of irregular verbs.

Exercise 1

Use the information about Michael Harris from the Task to complete the doctor's report about him. Use the simple past, simple present, or present perfect of the verbs in parentheses.

REPORT ON MICHAEL HARRIS

Michael Harris spoke with me yesterday about serious headaches. He (1) _____ (have) these headaches for two months. His previous medical history is good. He (2) _____ (not have) any serious illnesses. In 1973, he (3) _____ (be) in the hospital for three weeks, when he (4) _____ (break) both legs in a car accident. He (5) _____ (not smoke) now; he (6) _____ (stop) ten years ago, and he (7) _____ (not smoke) since that time. He (8) _____ (wear) glasses for reading, and he (9) _____ (wear) them since 1987. He (10) _____ (drink) a little wine with dinner every night. I examined Mr. Harris and took several tests. I asked him to return next week.

Exercise 2

Write the questions that the doctor asked Mr. Harris in order to get these responses.

EXAMPLE: 1 *Do you drink?*

Yes, a little. I drink a glass of wine with dinner every night.

2. _____?

Yes, I do. I wear them for reading.

3. _____?

I started wearing them in 1987.

4. _____?

Yes, I've worn them since 1987.

5. _____?

No, I don't smoke now.

6. _____?

I stopped ten years ago.

7. _____?

No, I haven't smoked since that time.

8. _____?

Yes, I have had these headaches for two months.

Exercise 3

Go back to Exercises 1 and 2. Look for the words *since* and *for*.

In the boxes below, write down the word or words that directly follow them. We have done the first one for you.

Since	For
	two months

What does this tell you about the use of *since* and *for*?

Focus 3

MEANING

For versus Since

MEANING

- You can use *for* to talk about the **length** of a period of time (for two weeks; for ten years; for five minutes).
- You can use *since* to talk about **when** a period of time **began** (since 1985; since my birthday; since Monday; since April).

Focus 4

For and Since

- You can use *since* to introduce a time clause:

Main Clause (from past to present)	Time Clause (past)
(a) He has worked here	**since** he graduated from high school.

- You can also use *since* with a phrase referring to a specific time:
  - **(b)** He has worked here **since** April.
  - **(c)** He has worked here **since** the beginning of the month.
- You can use *for* with a phrase that refers to a quantity of time, but not with a time clause:
  - **(d)** He has worked here **for** several years.
- It is possible to omit *for*:
  - **(e)** I've lived here five months.
  - **(f)** I've lived here **for** five months.

  Both **(e)** and **(f)** are correct; **(e)** is more informal.
- It is also also possible to omit *for* in questions:
  - **(g)** (**For**) how long have you lived here?
- It is not possible to omit *since*:
  - **(h)** I've lived here **since** January.
    NOT: I've lived here January.
  - **(i)** **Since** when have you lived here?
    NOT: When have you lived here?

Exercise 4

What difference in meaning (if any) is there in these statements?

1. He lived here for ten years.
   He has lived here for ten years.
2. (It is May. He moved here three months ago.)
   He has lived here for three months.
   He has lived here since February.
3. They have worked for the same company for a long time.
   They worked for the same company for a long time.

4. She has known them many years.
   She has known them for many years.

5. (It is July.)
   Anthony hasn't smoked for six months.
   Anthony stopped smoking in January.

Exercise 5

Look at the hotel register. How many people are staying in the hotel right now? Who has stayed there the longest?

Hotel Beresford Arms

701 Polk Street ▪ San Francisco, CA 94109
(415) 493-0443

Date: *3/11*

Guest	Check-In	Check-Out
Mr. Cruise	3/3	
B. Simpson	3/1	
Mr. and Mrs. Kowlowski	3/8	
Mr. and Mrs. Gordon	3/2	3/5
Ms. Chapman	3/2	
Mr. Nixon	3/2	3/8
Maria da Costa	3/6	
Yee Mun Ling	3/4	

Use the information from the register to make statements with the words given below.

1. Mr. and Mrs. Gordon / for
2. Maria da Costa / since
3. Yee Mun Ling / since
4. Mr. B. Simpson / for
5. Mr. and Mrs. Kolowski / for
6. Ms. Chapman / since
7. Mr. Cruise / for
8. Mr. Nixon / for

121

Exercise 6

Read the following statements and decide if they are referring to an action that is finished or unfinished. If you think it is finished, write *F* beside it; write *U* if you think it is unfinished.

1. He has lived here 20 years.
2. We have studied English for a few months.
3. I saw him last week.
4. My friends worked there for six months.
5. He's worn glasses since he was a child.
6. She slept ten hours.

Focus 5

USE

Actions Continuing Up to Now

USE

- When you talk about the duration of an action or situation that began in the past and that continues to the present, you can use **present perfect +** *for* or *since* **+ time word or phrase.**

    (a) They **have studied** martial arts for a long time.

    (b) Carrie **has been** a member of the tennis club since May.

- Some verbs are not used in this way because the actions they describe cannot continue from past to present.

    (c) Shin **started** to smoke on his eighteenth birthday, so he has smoked **for** three years.

    (d) NOT: He has started to smoke for three years.

    In **(c)**, we understand that it is the smoking that continues, not the starting. *Start* refers to something that happens at one time only, or at several different times, but not to an action that continues over time.

- For the same reason, the following verbs are not usually used with **present perfect +** *for* or ***since*** to express the duration of an action or situation that continues from past to present:

start	*leave*
arrive	*meet*
begin	*stop*

Exercise 7

Rewrite these sentences using the present perfect and *since* or *for*.

   EXAMPLE: Karen wears glasses. She started to wear glasses when she was a child.
   Karen has worn glasses since she was a child.

1. He works for the TV station. He started working there eight years ago.
2. They are married. They got married in 1962.
3. She knows how to fix a car. She learned how to do it a long time ago.
4. Tom rides his bike to work. He started to do it when his car broke down.
5. I wanted to go to China several years ago. I still want to go now.
6. My brother stopped smoking when he was in college, and he doesn't smoke now.
7. I was afraid of bats when I was a child, and I am afraid of them now.
8. My mother is in France. She went there last week.
9. My sister runs two miles every morning before breakfast. She started to do this when she was 15 years old.
10. They go to Cape Cod every summer. They started to do this 12 years ago.

Exercise 8

Complete the following. Put in the empty blanks *since* or *for* or the appropriate form of the verb in parentheses.

   Leroy and Paula are having a party. Two of their guests, Lee and Bob, have just met.

Lee: (1) *Have you known* (know) Leroy and Paula (2) *for* a long time?

Bob: I (3) _____ (know) Paula (4) _____ my senior year in

college. I first (5) _____ (meet) Leroy at their wedding two years ago. What

about you?

Lee: I'm a colleague of Leroy's. We (6) _____ (work) together

(7) _____ several years.

Bob: Oh, Leroy (8) _____ (show) me some of your work last week. It's great.

Lee: Thanks. What do you do?

Bob: I (9) _____ (teach) French (10) _____ ten years, but I

(11) _____ (quit) a couple of years ago. Now I'm an actor.

Lee: An actor! I thought you looked familiar.

Bob: Well, not really. I (12) _____ (not work) as an actor (13) _____ last

October. In fact, last night I (14) _____ (start) to work as a waiter at the

Zenon.

Lee: Really? I (15) _____ (eat) there last night. *That's* why you look familiar!

Exercise 9

Look at the following and underline the sentences that you think are correct.

My sister is very good at languages.

1. She studies Italian; she started studying Italian in 1991, so . . .

   she has studied Italian for several years.
   she studies Italian several years.
   she studied Italian for several years.
   she is studying Italian since 1991.

2. When she was a child, she wanted to learn Russian; she still wants to learn it.

   She has wanted to learn Russian when she was a child.
   She wants to learn Russian since she has been a child.
   She has wanted to learn Russian for she was a child.
   She has wanted to learn Russian since she was a child.

3. Two years ago she started taking courses at the local community college. Unfortunately, she doesn't have a car, so . . .

   she takes the bus to school for two years.
   she have taken the bus to school for two years.
   she has taken the bus to school since two years.
   she has taken the bus to school for two years.

Activities

Activity 1

Work in pairs or groups of three. Complete the following with information about your partner(s). You will need to decide on appropriate questions to ask before you start. For example:

How long have you studied English?

How long have you lived in this town?

1. _____ for _____ hours.

2. _____ since _____.

3. _____ for _____.

4. _____ for _____ years.

5. _____ since _____.

Activity 2

Work with a partner. Read the statements below and try to match each statement to people in your class. Write the name in the column marked *Guesses*. Next, verify your guesses by asking people if your guess is right or wrong.

GUESSES	WHO ...	FACTS
_____	has studied English the longest time?	_____
_____	has been married the longest time?	_____
_____	has owned his or her watch the longest time?	_____
_____	has known how to drive the longest time?	_____
_____	has known how to drive the shortest time?	_____
_____	has had the shoes she or he is wearing today the longest time?	_____
_____	has smoked the longest time?	_____
_____	has worn glasses the longest time?	_____
_____	has worn glasses the shortest time?	_____
_____	has had the same hairstyle the longest time?	_____

Activity 3

Political Power

In this activity, you will be finding out how different countries are governed. Get together with a group of classmates from different countries, if possible. First use the chart to think about your own country or a country you are familiar with. When you have all had enough time to think, begin sharing your information. Use the chart to take notes on what your classmates tell you. In the first part of the chart, check (✔) the appropriate box or write in the box marked *other*. In the second part of the chart, write notes. Be ready to share this information with the rest of the class.

Country	Type of Leadership				
	President	Monarch*	Prime Minister	Military	Other
Great Britain		✔	✔		

*king, queen, emperor, etc.

Country	How Current Leader Came into Power			
	Election	Succession	Coup	Other
Great Britain	✔ *(Prime minister)*	✔ *(Queen)*		

Country	Length of Time the Current Leader Has Been in Power	Best Thing She or He Has Done While in Power	Worst Thing She or He Has Done While in Power**

**If you don't want to talk about your country's leader, you can talk about the President of the United States.

Present Perfect and Simple Past

Ever and *Never*

Task

Work with a partner and quickly read this page from Max's passport. How many different countries has Max visited? When did he visit each one?

Now use Max's passport to complete the following:

Max has visited (1) _____ countries in Asia, Europe, and North America. He has

been to (2) _____ different countries in Asia. He went to (3) _____

and Malaysia in (4) _____ . He went to Singapore in (5) _____ ,

and he went to Indonesia in (6) _____ . He has been to (7) _____

twice. The first time he went there was in (8) _____ , and the second time

was in (9) _____ . He also went to Taiwan in (10) _____ .

In addition, he has visited (11) _____ countries in Europe. He went to

(12) _____ in 1985 and England in (13) _____ . Max has also been

to (14) _____ ; he went there in (15) _____ . Although he has

been to many different countries in his life, he hopes to visit many more in the future.

Focus 1

Present Perfect
versus Simple Past

USE

- To talk about a completed action, experience, or situation at a **specific time** in the past, you
  can use simple past to show that you are thinking about the **past**, not the present:
  (a) Last year, she **graduated** from high school.

LAST YEAR

NOW

(b) He **lived** in this house from 1980 to 1988.

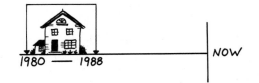

- To talk about a completed action, experience, or situation in the past when **you do not refer to when it happened**, use present perfect:

(c) He **has been** to Mexico.

(d) They **have run** a marathon.

- Here we show that something happened in the past, but we do not show **when** it happened. We show only that it happened **at some time before now**; we are thinking about the past in relation to the present:

  (e) I **drank** champagne last night. (**simple past** because I want to show **when** it happened)

  (f) I **have drunk** champagne. (**present perfect** because I want to show that **the experience** is more important than when I did it)

- We often use the present perfect to introduce the general idea and then continue with the simple past to give specific details about it:

  (g) **I've been** to Thailand. I **went** there about ten years ago and traveled all over the country. I **had** a great time, and I **enjoyed** meeting the friendly Thai people.

Exercise 1

Turn back to the Task. Circle every marker of past time (in 1975, 10 years ago, and so on) you can find. Now draw a line connecting this time word with a verb. Is the verb simple past or present perfect? Why do you think this is so?

Focus 2

FORM

Forming the Present Perfect

 FORM

- You form the present perfect with *has/have* + past participle:
  - **(a)** Rob and Barbara **have seen** that movie.
  - **(b)** Carolyn **hasn't written** to me.
  - **(c) Have** you **eaten** oysters?
  - **(d)** Tessa **has visited** a lot of different countries.
- For more information on forming the present perfect, see Unit 11, Focus 2.

Exercise 2

There is a "classic" film festival in town featuring a number of famous American movies. Robert loves classic movies, and so he is is planning to invite some friends to a movie on Saturday night. Naturally, he wants to suggest a movie that nobody has seen. Use the information below to help him choose.

FILM FESTIVAL

BALBOA
38th & Balboa 221–8184
- HIGH NOON
    4:55   8:30   10:55
- ROMAN HOLIDAY
    6:50   10:25
- PSYCHO
    12:30   4:45   8:40   11:15

CORONET
Geary & Arguelio, 752–4400
- ON THE WATERFRONT
    1:20   3:30   5:37   7:30

GALAXY
Van Ness & Sutter 474–8700
- THE GODFATHER
    6:10   8:30   10:55

METRO
Union-Webster 931–1835
- CASABLANCA
    1:00   3:15   5:30   10:00

REGENCY
Van Ness & Sutter 585–6773
- THE GRADUATE
    4:40   7:40   10:30

---

1. Ann has seen the movie at the Coronet.
2. Patty and Mark went to the Metro last night.
3. Karen went to the Balboa on Tuesday to see the movie that started at 8:30.
4. Tom went to the Galaxy last weekend.
5. Carolyn and Terry have seen the movie at the Regency.
6. A couple of days ago Robert went to the Balboa and saw the movie that started at 8:40.

Which movie should they go and see?
Have **you** seen any of these movies?
Find out how many of your classmates have seen these movies.

Exercise 3

Use the information from the last exercise to make appropriate questions for the following responses.

EXAMPLE: *Did Carolyn & Terry go to the movies yesterday* _____?

Yes, they did. They went to see *The Graduate* yesterday.

1. _____?

Yes. Tom has seen *The Godfather.*

2. _____?

No, Patty and Mark haven't seen *High Noon.*

3. _____?

No, she didn't see it last weekend. She saw it on Tuesday.

4. _____?

No, they didn't see *Psycho.* They saw *Casablanca.*

5. _____?

Yes, he has. He saw it a couple of days ago.

6. _____?

No, they haven't seen *Roman Holiday*, but they have seen *The Graduate.*

7. _____?

No, he didn't. He saw it last weekend.

Exercise 4

Alice is on vacation in New York City. Complete her postcard home, using either simple past or present perfect with the verbs in parentheses.

Hi folks!

Having a great time! I (1) _____ (walk) at least 50 miles, but I (2) _____ (see) lots of interesting things. Yesterday I (3) _____ (take) the Staten Island Ferry, and on Thursday I (4) _____ (go) to the top of the Empire State Building. I (5) _____ (see) several shows. Two nights ago I (6) _____ (go) to see Cats: I (7) _____ (have) great tickets. Wonderful food!!! I (8) _____ (eat) some delicious meals. Yesterday I (9) _____ (try) sushi for the first time.

See you next week.

Love, Alice

P.S. I (10) _____ (spend) lots of money!

The Murphys
1403 Eastwood
Ann Arbor,
MI 48103

19¢

Exercise 5

Read this job advertisement:

What kind of job do you think this is?

EXCITING OPPORTUNITY
for the right person
Are you independent
and adventurous?
Requirements:
* knowledge of other cultures
* ability to speak at least one
foreign language
* flexibility
* must enjoy working with other
people and like travel.
Interested?
This is a difficult but
well-paying job.
Write Box 392,
giving a short description of your
previous experience.

This is one of the letters the company received in answer to the advertisement. Complete the blanks with the appropriate form of the verb in parentheses. The first one has been for you.

Dear Sir,

I am writing about the job advertised in today's paper.

I (1) _graduated_ (graduate) from high school in 1978. I (2) _____ (have) experience in many different fields. I (3) _____ (work) as a typist, receptionist, sales assistant, and teacher. I (4) _____ (travel) extensively and (5) _____ (learn) Spanish, French, and Italian.

In 1979, I (6) _____ (go) to Europe. First I (7) _____ (work) as a tour guide and (8) _____ (help) American tourists in Paris, France. After that, I (9) _____ (move) to Italy, where I (10) _____ (live) with an Italian family and (11) _____ (look after) their three children. In 1984, I (12) _____ (work) in Barcelona, Spain, for three months and (13) _____ (teach) English conversation to children. In 1985, I (14) _____ (return) to the United States, and I (15) _____ (be) a receptionist at a beauty salon for six months. In 1986, I (16) _____ (leave) the United States again, and for two years I (17) _____ (give) sailing lessons on charter yachts in the Caribbean. I finally (18) _____ (come) home to the United States in 1989 and (19) _____ (take) a job at City Bookstore.

As you can see, I (20) _____ (work) with a lot of different people, and I (21) _____ (experience) different cultures. In all my jobs, I (22) _____ (enjoy) meeting other people. I believe this experience makes me a good candidate for the job.

Sincerely,

Nancy Martin

Nancy Martin

Do *you* think Nancy Martin is a good candidate for the job? Why do you think so?

Focus 3

Ever and *Never*

MEANING

- *Ever* with the present perfect tense means "at any time before now." It is usually used in questions and negative statements. It is not usually used in affirmative statements:

   (a) Have you **ever eaten** Mexican food?

       Yes, I **have eaten** Mexican food.

       NOT: I have ever eaten Mexican food.

   (b) I **haven't ever** eaten Mexican food.

- *Never* with the present perfect tense means "at no time before now":

   (c) I **have never eaten** Mexican food.

- *Not* versus *never*

   - These sentences have similar meanings:

      (d) I **have never eaten** Mexican food.

      (e) I **have not eaten** Mexican food.

   - *Never* means *not* + *ever*. In sentence (d), *never* emphasizes the fact that I have not had this experience in my life before the present moment. It is therefore stronger than *not*.

Exercise 6

Read the conversation. Underline and correct any mistakes.

Mick: Have you ever <u>visit</u> Europe?   *visited*

Dave: Yes. I've been there several times, in fact. Three years ago I've gone to France.

Mick: Really? Where did you go?

Dave: I went to Paris, of course. And then I rode my mountain bike in the Pyrenees. Last year I've ridden my bike in Germany and Switzerland. Have ever you been there?

Mick: I've never been to Germany, but I've ever been to Switzerland.

Dave: When was that?

Mick: I've studied German there about eight years ago.

Focus 4

Present Perfect versus Simple Past: Questions

USE

- When you ask the question, "Have you ever eaten frogs' legs?" you are interested in knowing about the experience, not about when it happened. You expect the answer: "Yes, I have," "No, I haven't," or "No, I've never done that."
- When you ask, "When did you eat them?" you are more interested in when it happened, and we expect the answer to tell us about that: "Two years ago" or "I ate them two years ago."

Exercise 7

Complete the conversations, using the present perfect or the past simple of the verbs in parentheses. The first one has been done for you.

1. **A:** Excuse me, sir, we're doing a survey. Can I ask you a few questions?

   B: Sure, go ahead.

   A: *Have you ever used* WonderWhite detergent? (you/use/ever)

   B: No, _____ it. (I/try/never)

   A: Why not?

   B: _____ laundry in my life. (I/do/never) My wife always does it.

   A: What about you, sir? _____ your clothes with WonderWhite?

   (you/wash/ever)

   C: Yes, _____ it. (I/try)

   A: When _____ it for the first time? (you/try)

   C: _____ it for the first time about six months ago. (I/use)

2. **A:** _____ any books by Latin American writers? (you/read/ever)

   B: Yes, I _____ . I _____ a great novel by a Colombian writer a few years ago. (read)

   A: Which one?

   B: I _____ his name.(forget) He _____ the Nobel Prize several years ago. (win)

   A: Oh, you mean Gabriel Garcia Marquez.

3. **A:** My brother is coming to stay with us for a few days next week. Do you have any ideas about how we can entertain him?

   B: _____ here before now? (he/be/ever)

   A: Yes. He _____ (come) once about three years ago.

   B: _____ to Chinatown then? (he/go)

   A: No _____ Chinatown (he/be/never), but _____ a lot in China and in the Far East. (he/travel)

   B: Maybe you'd better not take him to Chinatown then! _____ him to Greek-town when he was here three years ago? (you/take)

   A: No, and _____ Greece (he/visit/never).

   B: Great! Why don't you take him there?

4. **A:** _____ last night? (you/ go out)

   B: Yes. _____ to that new Italian restaurant. (we/go)

   A: What's it like? _____ there. (I/be/never)

   B: It's O.K., but _____ better Italian food in other restaurants. (I/eat)

   A: _____ the one on Main Street? (you/try/ever)

   B: Yes. _____ great meal there last weekend. (we/have)

Exercise 8

Complete the following, using the words in parentheses.

My friend and I (1) _____ (decide) to take our next vacation in Bali. Yesterday we (2) _____ (go) to a travel agent and we (3) _____ (pick up) lots of different brochures. We (4) _____ (take) them home and (5) _____ (read) them all very carefully. We want to go there because my friend (6) _____ (travel) in Southeast Asia, but she (7) _____ (never be) to Bali and I (8) _____ (read) many books about the customs and culture of the Balinese people. My brother (9) _____ (be) there several times. He (10) _____ (go) there for the first time about 15 years ago, and he (11) _____ (stay) there for six months. He (12) _____ (return) to Bali last year and according to him, life there (13) _____ (change) a lot because there are so many tourists now. I don't care! I (14) _____ (hear) so many different things about Bali, but now I want to find out for myself!

Activities

Activity 1

In this activity, you will be finding out about some of the things that your classmates have done. Look at the list below. Move around the class and ask questions to see if you can find anyone who has ever done any of these things.

First you need to find who has had the experience (name); then you need to get specific details about the experience (when) (where) (how/why). Take notes below; it is not necessary to write full sentences at this point. In the box marked ★★★, you can add a question of your own if you want to.

Be ready to share your findings with the rest of the class. Finally, you will use this information to make a written report.

HAVE YOU EVER ...?

Experience	Name	When	Where	How/Why
met a famous person				
climbed a mountain				
seen a shark				
felt really frightened				
flown in a hot-air balloon				
★★★				

Now use the information you collected to complete this report on your findings.

A few days ago I interviewed some of my classmates about things they have done before now, and I learned some interesting things about their past experiences. For example,....

Activity 2

Move around the class and ask questions to find out if the following statements are true or false. If the statement is true, write *T* beside it; if it is false, write *F*.

1. Somebody in this room has appeared on TV.
2. Everybody here has eaten tacos.
3. At least three people have never ridden on a motorcycle.
4. Somebody has swum in more than two oceans.
5. Several people have seen a ghost.
6. At least three people have been to Disneyland.
7. Nobody has been to Paris.
8. Somebody has run a marathon.
9. Half the class has never played soccer.
10. Somebody has never smoked a cigarette.

Activity 3

The purpose of this activity is to confuse your classmates. You will tell the class about three things you have done in your life. Two of these things are true, but one is false. Your classmates will try to guess which one is false. For example:

I have ridden a bicycle from San Francisco to Los Angeles.

I have traveled by boat up the Amazon.

I have broken my leg twice.

Which statement is false?

In order to decide which one is false, your classmates can ask you questions about the specific details of each experience. For example, "When did you ride your bike to Los Angeles?" "How long did it take?" "Which leg did you break?" and so on. After they have listened to your answers, the class will vote on which experience is false.

Take turns talking about your true and false experiences until everyone has taken part.

Activity 4

You have probably had many different experiences since you came to this country. In this activity you will be finding out the best and the worst experiences your classmates have had since they came here. First go around the room and get as much information as you can from at least three different people. Use the chart to take notes on the information your classmates give you.

Name	Country	Length of Time She or He Has Been Here	Best Experience	Worst Experience

You have been asked to write a short article for your college newspaper on the experiences of foreign students.

Review the information you collected and choose the two most interesting or surprising "best" experiences and the two most interesting or surprising "worst" experiences. Organize your article so that you talk first about the bad experiences and then about the good experiences. Start your article with a brief introduction to the topic and to the students you interviewed. For example:

> What is it like to be a foreign student? I will try to answer this question by telling you about both the good and bad experiences of some of my classmates. Recently I interviewed (number) students in my class and they told me about the best and the worst times they have had since they came here. I would like to share with you some of the things I learned.

Activity 5

Write a letter to a family member or a friend and tell him or her about the best and the worst experiences you have had since you left home.

142

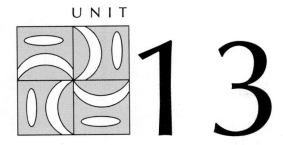

U N I T

13

Present Perfect
Progressive

Task

Read the statements below. Why do you think they were said? What had probably happened just before?

STATEMENT	RECENT ACTIVITY

1. **A:** Ugh.... your hands are covered
   with oil and grease!
   B: Sorry.
   _____

2. **A:** Are you O.K.? Your eyes are all red. _____

3. **A:** You look terrible.
   B: I didn't get much sleep last night.
   _____

4. **A:** That's enough for tonight. Give me
   your car keys.
   B: Why?
   A: I'll take you home. You can't drive
   like this.
   _____

5. **A:** Why is your hair wet? _____

6. **A:** Hey, kids! Stop right there!
   B: What for?
   A: Take your shoes off at once! I don't
   want mud all over the carpet.
   _____

Now look at the activities in the list. Try to match each of the statements above to an appropriate activity in the list. Write the activity in the space beside the statement.

ACTIVITIES

baking bread
swimming
chopping onions
eating garlic
playing in the yard

drinking
studying for a test
running
fixing a car
watching TV

143

Focus 1

Present Perfect Progressive: Recent Activity

MEANING
USE

- The present perfect progressive connects the past with the present in two slightly different ways. You can use the present perfect progressive to talk about an activity which was in progress very recently in the past:

I'VE BEEN PAINTING MY ROOM.

(a) Why are your hands green?
I've **been painting** my room.

- The activity is so recent that its effect or result is often still visible or apparent in the present.

Focus 2

FORM

Present Perfect Progressive

FORM

- *has/have + been +* verb *+ -ing:*

Statement	Negative	Question
I You } **have been sleeping.** We ('ve) They	I You } **have not been sleeping.** We (**haven't**) They	**Have** { I you we they } **been sleeping?**
She } He } **has been sleeping.** It ('s)	She } He } **has not been sleeping.** It (**hasn't**)	**Has** { she he it } **been sleeping?**

Exercise 1

Turn back to the Task and write appropriate statements, using the present perfect progressive in response to statements 1–6. The first one has been done for you:

1. *She has been fixing a car* _____.

2. _____.

3. _____.

4. _____.

5. _____.

6. _____.

Exercise 2

You are riding the subway in a big city, late at night. There are several other people in the same car. You observe them carefully and try to figure out what they have been doing recently. Probably you will be able to think of several possibilities for each one.

1. A young man with a black eye and ripped clothing:

   He _____.

2. A man with lipstick traces on his face and on the collar of his shirt:

   He _____.

3. Two young women with many bags and packages from well-known department stores:

   They _____.

4. A couple wearing shorts and walking shoes and carrying backpacks. They seem very tired:

   They _____.

5. A young woman with a bookbag full of chemistry textbooks. She has a book open in her hands and she is asleep:

   She _____.

6. A woman with red stains on her hands:

She _____.

7. A man with white hairs all over his clothes and scratches on his hands.

He _____.

Focus 3

Actions Continuing
to the Present

• We also use the present perfect progressive to describe actions or situations starting in the past and continuing up to and including now.

(a) He has been waiting for 20 minutes (and he is still waiting).

Exercise 3

Complete the following sentences, using the "scrambled" verb in parentheses. We have done the first one for you.

1.   **Lee:**   What are you doing?

 Mary Lou: I'm waiting to make a phone call. This woman *has been talking* on the

    phone for the last 20 minutes. (katl)

2. **Dan:**   Haven't you finished writing that book yet?

  Heidi: No, we're still working on it.

   Dan: You _____ it for almost a year! (retwi)

  Heidi: I know, but it's nearly finished now.

3. **Sky:** What's up? You look miserable.

   Tom: I am. I want to go for a bike ride, but it _____ since eight o'clock this morning. (anir)

4. **Gin:** What do you want to do tonight?

   Bruce: I want to go out and have fun. I _____ here all day. (krow)

5. **George:** Excuse me, but is this your dog?

   Barbara: Yes. Is there a problem?

   George: I can't get to sleep because that dog _____ for hours! Please keep it under control, or I'll call the police. (krab)

6. **Julie:** Have you seen Patsy recently?

   Jan: No. She's got a new boyfriend, and she _____ all her time with him. (psned)

7. **John:** Are these your glasses?

   Betty: Yes! Thank you so much. I _____ for them everywhere! (oklo)

8. **Mike:** How are things going in New York?

   Dave: We don't live there anymore.

   Mike: Really?

   Dave: Yes. We _____ in Philadelphia since January. (lvei)

9. **Diane:** Why are Kemal and Cynthia so depressed?

   Marianne: They _____ grammar for ages, but they still don't understand how to use the present perfect progressive. (yusdt)

10. **Pam:** Aren't you ready yet?

    Andrew: No. I've lost my keys and I _____ to find them for the last half hour. (ytr)

Focus 4

Present Perfect Progressive versus Present Perfect

USE

- The **present perfect** and the **present perfect progressive** can both describe actions or situations starting in the past and continuing up to and including now. In this case, it is necessary to add a time adverbial to show how long the activity has been in progress:

  (a) Jim has worked here **for ten years.**

  (b) Jim has been working here **for ten years.**

  In both sentences, we understand that Jim still works here.

- The following verbs are commonly used with both present perfect and present perfect progressive to describe an unfinished action:

  live   work   teach   study

- You can also use the present perfect progressive to **emphasize** an activity that started in the past and that continues **without interruption** to the present:

  (c) We **have been working** on this for a long time.

- You can express the same meaning with the present perfect:

  (d) We **have worked** on this for a long time.

- The present perfect progressive emphasizes the fact that the activity has continued without stopping.

- The present perfect **without a time adverbial** shows that an activity finished sometime before now in the past, but we are not sure when:

  (e) They **have painted** their house.

- As you saw in Focus 1, the present perfect progressive without a time adverbial is often used to talk about an activity that finished very recently before now:

  (f) They **have been painting** their house.

- See Unit 12 for more information on this use of the present perfect.

Exercise 4

Look at each group of statements and discuss the differences in meaning. Think of a possible situation in which you could use each statement.

1. **a.** Bill has read that book.
   b. Bill has been reading that book.
   c. Bill has been reading that book for three weeks.
2. **a.** Sally has eaten frogs' legs.
   b. Sally has been eating frogs' legs.
3. **a.** I've been riding a motorcycle.
   b. I've ridden a motorcycle.
   c. I've ridden a motorcycle since I was a teenager.
4. **a.** We've been studying English grammar.
   b. We've studied English grammar.
   c. We've been studying English grammar for a long time.
   d. We've studied English grammar for a long time.

Focus 5

USE

Recent Habits

USE

- You can also use the present perfect progressive to talk about a regular habit or activity that someone started recently and which she or he continues to do. In this situation, you can add a time adverbial to emphasize that the action started recently:
  - **(a)** They've been eating out a lot **recently.**
  - **(b)** He's been working a lot **lately.**
  - **(c)** I've been walking to work **recently.**
  - **(d)** I've walked to work.
- In (c), we understand that "walking to work" is a recent habit. I started to do this a short time ago and will continue in the future.
- In (d), we understand that I did this at some time in the past, but I do not do it at the moment. In this situation, you do not usually add a time adverbial.

149

Exercise 5

Barbara is talking with her old friend, Janet. They have not seen each other for several months, and Janet is surprised by some of the changes in Barbara's appearance. Complete their conversation, using verbs from the list below.

happen	sail	cook
do	feel	take
go	study	eat
ride	date	ski
talk		

Janet: Barbara, you look great! You've really lost a lot of weight.

Barbara: Well, I (1) _____ my bike to school recently and I

(2) _____ an aerobics class.

Janet: Is that all? No special diets or anything?

Barbara: Not really. I (3) _____ (not) to any fast-food restaurants, and I

(4) _____ at home instead. So I (5) _____ a lot of

fresh vegetables and salads and other healthy stuff like that. It really makes a difference. I

(6) _____ much better, with lots more energy.

Janet: Well, you seem to be very busy these days. You're never home when I call. What else

(7) _____ you _____ ?

Barbara: I (8) _____ this really cute guy. He has a boat, so we

(9) _____ a lot and he also has a cabin in the mountains, so we

(10) _____ too. And also, we (11) _____

about taking some trips together. So it's all pretty exciting. But what about you? What

(12) _____ with you?

Janet: Nothing. I (13) _____ for my final exams, but when they're over,

I'm going to start having fun!

Exercise 6

What would Holly and Don say in each situation below? The words in parentheses will help you, but you will need to add some other words of your own.

1. It's 4:00, and Holly's husband Don has been napping since 1:00. Holly is waiting for him to wake up. When he finally wakes up, she says: (I/wait/three hours)

   _____

   _____ .

2. Don has promised to change the oil in Holly's car. While he is sleeping, she decides to try to do it herself, but she can't. When Don wakes up, she says: (I/try/45 minutes)

   _____

   _____ .

3. Holly's mother calls to tell her that Holly's sister has had another baby. Her mother asks, "When are you and Don going to have kids?" Holly tells her: (we/discuss/ten years)

   _____

   _____ .

4. After his nap, Don is hungry and he wants Holly to go out with him to eat pizza. Holly doesn't want to go because she bought fresh fish for dinner and wants to try out a new recipe. She tells Don, "I don't want to go out to eat because (I/plan/dinner/all day)"

   _____

   _____ .

Exercise 7

Complete the dialogues, using present perfect progressive, present perfect, or simple past. Be prepared to explain your choice.

Jim: What's the matter? You look frustrated.

Jill: I am. I (1) _____ (try) to study all day, but the telephone never

stops ringing. People (2) _____ (call) all day about the car.

Jim: That's great. I (3) _____ (hope) to sell that car for six months now.

Maybe today's the day!

Maria: I'm sorry I'm so late. (4) _____ (you/wait) long?

Alex: Yes, I have! Where (5) _____ (you/be)?

Maria: I really am sorry. My watch is broken, and I didn't know what time it was.

Alex: Why didn't you ask somebody? I (6) _____ (stand) out here in the

cold for at least 40 minutes.

Maria: Oh, you poor thing! But we'd better hurry to get to the movie theater.

Alex: It's too late. The movie (7) _____ (start).

Maria: Really?

Alex: Yes. It (8) _____ (start) 20 minutes ago.

Activities

Activity 1

You have just received a letter from the editor of your high school newspaper. She wants to include information about former students in the next edition of the paper. Write a letter to the editor, telling her what you have been doing recently. (Do not feel you have to use present perfect progressive in every sentence! To make this a natural letter, think about all the other tenses you can use as well.)

Activity 2

WHAT HAVE I BEEN DOING?
The purpose of this game is to guess recent activities from their current results.
Work in teams. Each team should try to think of four different results of recent activities. An example of one of these could be

Recent Activity   **Present Result**
You have been exercising and now you are exhausted.

When everyone is ready, each team takes turns to pantomime the results of the activities they have chosen. For example, Team A has chosen "being exhausted." Everybody in Team A gets up and pantomimes being exhausted. The rest of the class tries to guess what Team A has been doing. The first person to guess correctly, "You have been exercising and now you are exhausted," scores a point for his or her team.

Activity 3

This is another team game. Each team presents a series of clues, and the rest of the class try to guess what situation these clues refer to. For example, Team A chooses this situation: A woman has been reading a sad love story. The team tries to think of as many clues as possible that will help the other students guess the situation. When everyone is ready, Team A presents the first clue:

Team A: Her eyes are red.

The other teams make guesses based on this first clue:

Team B: She has been chopping onions.
Team A: No. She feels very sad.
Team C: She's been crying.
Team A: No. She's very romantic.
Team D: She's been fighting with her boyfriend.
Team A: No. She was alone while she was doing this.
Team C: She's been reading a sad love story.

You can choose one of the situations below or you can choose one of your own.

1. She or he has been crying.
2. She or he has been watching old movies.
3. She or he has been coughing a lot.
4. She or he's been training for the Olympics.
5. She or he has been chopping onions.
6. She or he has been feeling sick.
7. She or he has been losing weight.

The person who guesses the correct situation scores a point for his or her team.

Activity 4

Describe some things that you have been doing since you came to this country that you had never done before. Share your experiences with your classmates. Make a poster depicting everybody's experiences.

Activity 5

Listen to a news broadcast. What events have been happening in the world? What are some important events that have happened in the last five years?

UNIT

14

Making Offers with
Would...Like

Task

Imagine that you are at a party. Your friend is on the other side of the room. You can see each other, but you cannot hear each other because the room is very crowded and the music is very loud.

For this activity, work in pairs. Student A: Communicate the problem (listed on the chart below) to Student B **without speaking or writing**. Student B: **Do not** look at the list of problems. Your job is to offer a solution to Student A **without speaking or writing**. You will both need to pantomime your responses to each other. That is, you will need to use gestures, facial expressions, and other nonverbal ways of communicating.

When you have finished, check the list to see if Student B correctly understood Student A's problems. Then write down an appropriate *offer* using *Would you like?* . . . on the Solutions side of the chart.

Problems	Solutions
Student A: **1.** You are thirsty and want something to drink.	
2. You have a headache.	
3. You are hot. You want your friend to open a window.	
4. You are hungry. Your friend is standing by a table with food on it. You want him or her to get you something to eat.	
5. You have to sneeze. You need a handkerchief.	
6. You need a light for your cigarette.	
7. You need an ashtray.	
8. You are tired. You want your friend to give you a ride home.	

Focus 1

USE

How to Make Offers

USE

- When someone has a problem or needs something, there are several ways to offer help. The most polite way is to use *Would you like?* . . .

Focus 2

FORM

Different Ways to Make Offers

FORM

- There are several ways to make offers with *Would you like?* . . .
  - *Would you like* + noun phrase
    (a) Would you like some more coffee?
  - *Would you like to* + verb phrase
    (b) Would you like to sit down?
  - *Would you like me to* + verb phrase
    (c) Would you like me to open the window?
- This form is also useful when you make an offer about someone else.
  - *Would you like* (person) *to* + verb phrase
    (d) Would you like Sally to open the window?
    (e) Would you like someone to open the window?

Exercise 1

Look back at the offers you wrote down in the Task. Are your offers formed correctly?

Focus 3

Would You Like? . . .
versus *Do You Want?* . . .

USE

- *Would you like?* . . . is a polite way of asking *Do you want?* . . . . *Do you want?* . . . is an informal way of making an offer. Usually it is used with close friends and family. For example,

    (a) Would you like a cup of tea?

    is more polite than

    (b) Do you want a cup of tea?

    (c) Do you want me to help you with your homework?

    is more informal than

    (d) Would you like me to help you with your homework?

Exercise 2

Your new friend is having her first party in North America. She has invited some friends and their parents, but she has asked you to help her because she is nervous and does not know English very well. Change her following commands and questions into polite offers, using *Would you like?* . . .

1. Come in.
2. Sit down.
3. Give me your coat.
4. Want a chair?
5. Let me get you an ashtray.
6. Something to drink?
7. Cream in your coffee?
8. Want me to open that window for you?
9. More coffee?

DUANE GILLOGLY

Exercise 3

Look at the list below. Choose three things and make offers you hope your classmates will accept. Go around the class and make offers with *Would you like?...* to as many people as possible.

When you respond to an offer: a) be as polite as possible, and b) if you must refuse the offer, give a reason for refusing it.

1. listen to music
2. watch TV
3. eat something
4. drink something
5. borrow videos
6. read magazines
7. _____ (make up your own offer)

Exercise 4

Write down as many responses as you can remember to the offers that you made in Exercise 3. Write the responses of people who accepted your offer in the Accept column. Write the responses of people who refused your offer in the Refuse column. Then, for each column, rank these responses in order of politeness (Which responses seemed most polite? Which seemed least polite?)

Responses to Offers		
	Accept	**Refuse**
Most Polite ↑ ↓ **Least Polite**		

Focus 4

Politely Accepting and Refusing Offers

USE

- Using *please* along with *yes* is a polite way of accepting an offer.

Offer	Polite Acceptance
(a) Would you like something to drink?	Yes, please.

- Extra phrases that show that you appreciate the offer make your acceptance sound even more polite. But this is not always necessary in informal situations.

Offer	*Yes* + Appreciation
(b) Would you like me to help you?	Yes, please. That's very nice/kind of you.

- Using *thank you* or *thanks* along with *no* is a polite way of refusing an offer.

Offer	Polite Refusal
(c) Would you like some coffee?	No, thank you.
	No, thanks.

- Polite refusals can also include a reason why the offer cannot be accepted.

Offer	Refusal + Reason
(d) Would you like some coffee?	No, thank you. I've had enough.
(e) Would you like me to help you?	No, thanks. That's very nice of you, but I can manage.

Exercise 5

It is often difficult to refuse offers, especially when they are polite and sincere. Work with a partner for this exercise and take turns making offers and politely refusing them. Use the ideas in Exercise 3 to make offers, or make up your own. But this time all offers must be refused.

Exercise 6

Look at the following responses. What was the offer that was probably made? Write it down in the blank.

1. Offer: _____?

   Response: No, thanks. I've had enough.

2. Offer: _____?

   Response: Yes, please. It's delicious.

3. Offer: _____?

   Response: Oh, no, thank you. I've seen it already.

4. Offer: _____?

   Response: No, thanks. I'm warm enough.

5. Offer: _____?

   Response: Yes, please. It's very heavy.

6. Offer: _____?

   Response: Thanks, I'd love to. That sounds great.

7. Offer: _____?

   Response: Thanks, but I've already got one of my own.

Exercise 7

For each of the following situations, write a short dialogue in which one person makes a polite offer (using *Would . . . like*) and the other person either politely accepts or politely refuses the offer. Then find a partner and read your dialogues aloud, taking parts.

1. The English instructor, at the front of the classroom, is ready to show a video in class today. The switch to turn on the video player is right by Stefan, at the back of the room.

   Stefan says: _____?

   The instructor says: _____.

2. The dinner at Mrs. Black's house is almost finished. Mrs. Black notices that some of the guests ate their dessert—cherry pie—very quickly, and she thinks they might want another piece.

   Mrs. Black says: _____?

   A guest says: _____.

3. Alfredo has a seat at the front of the city bus. He notices that an old woman has just gotten on, but there are no more seats left.

   Alfredo says: _____?

   The old woman says: _____.

4. As Mary is about to leave for the post office, she sees that there are several envelopes on the desk, stamped and addressed by her roommate Judith.

   Mary says: _____?

   Judith says: _____.

5. Just as Thomas starts to drive away to work, he sees that his neighbor Rob is walking down the sidewalk to the bus stop. Thomas knows that Rob's office is not far from where he works.

   Thomas says: _____?

   Rob says: _____.

Activities

Activity 1

Your good friend is at home in bed, sick. You want to help out and make your friend feel better. Make a list of things that you might do to help and then make offers using *Would you like?* . . . . Your "friend" can accept or refuse your offers.

Activity 2

How do native speakers of English behave at parties? Is their behavior at formal parties different from their behavior at informal parties, where the guests are all close friends or relatives?

Complete the following chart and feel free to provide more information in the two blanks at the bottom. If you do not know the answers you need to complete the chart, find a native speaker of English or someone who has spent a long time in an English-speaking country. Interview him or her to get the information you need.

What Does the Host Do or Say When She or He:	Formal Parties	Informal Parties
(a) wants the guests to sit down		
(b) wants the guests to start eating		
(c) wants the guests to eat/drink more		
(d) wants the guests to start some activity (dancing/playing a game)		
(e)		
(f)		

Activity 3

How to Help Me
Take two pieces of paper. On each piece, write down one thing that a classmate could do for you that would be helpful. Write down something different on each piece. (If your class is a large group, one piece of paper is enough.) Hand in your pieces of paper and do not write your name on them.

Your teacher will give you two papers (one if it is a large class), which other students wrote, and you must decide who you think has written each request for help. Get up and go around the room to find that person. Make an offer to help him or her, using the *Would you like?...* form. If your offer is rejected, find someone else who you think wrote the original request for help.

You must accept an offer if it is about the help you requested (the thing you wrote down on your piece of paper). You must refuse all other offers for help, even if they sound good!

Activity 4

Without using any words, your group will mime a problem. (When you "mime," you use gestures, actions, and facial expressions to silently "act out" a situation. No words allowed!) Another group will try to guess what the problem is and make an appropriate offer to help solve the problem.

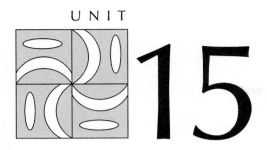

UNIT 15

Requests and Permission

Can/Could, Will/Would, May

Task

You are about to start house-sitting for a friend of yours. Your friend has left you a note with instructions about what to do while she is gone. Unfortunately, someone has spilled coffee on the note, and now it is difficult to read. Try to find the missing parts of the note from the choices on the next page. Write the appropriate number in the spaces on the note.

I'm glad you'll be here to watch the house while I'm gone! My neighbors think that this neighborhood is not completely safe at night, so (A)

The cats eat twice a day, (B)
I don't want them to stay out at night so (C)

The plants need to be watered twice a week. (D)

I left some bills to mail on the kitchen table. (E)

My cousin from out of town said that he would call this week. (F)

The rent check is on the kitchen table. It's due at the end of the week. (G)

I told the landlord about the broken light in the bathroom. If he calls, (H)

Thanks for everything. (I)

1. ... could you ask him to fix it as soon as possible?
2. ... remember to lock the windows and doors when it gets dark. Thanks.
3. ... so will you please give them water on Tuesday and Friday?
4. ... See you next week!
5. ... Would you mind mailing them for me tomorrow morning?
6. ... please make sure they come in around 8:00.
7. ... Would you take a message and tell him I'll be back on the 29th?
8. ... so could you feed them in the morning and at night?
9. ... Please mail it before Friday.

Focus 1

FORM ● USE

Making Polite Requests

FORM
USE

- Questions using the modals *can, could, will,* and *would* are ways of making polite requests. If you really want someone to say yes to a request, it is important to make the request polite.
  - The modals *could* and *would* sound more polite than the modals *can* and *will*.
  - Providing some good background or reason for why you are making the request and using *please* are also ways to make requests sound more polite. In questions, *please* **usually** comes between the subject *you* and the verb.
    (a) I left my notes at home. Could you **please** lend me yours?
  - The reason for making the request can also come **after** the question.
    (b) Could you please lend me your notes? I left mine at home.
  - Another way to make a polite request is to use the phrase *Would you mind* + verb + *-ing.*
    (c) Would you mind lending me your notes?

Exercise 1

Below are some situations in which requests are commonly made. For each situation, make a polite request.

1. You want to know what time it is. You find someone who is wearing a watch and you say: ____

_____ ?

2. When you pay for your groceries at the supermarket, you remember that you need some

change. You hand the cashier a dollar and say: _____

_____ ?

3. You have been waiting in line at the bank for 15 minutes, but you need to get a drink of water.

You turn to the friendly-looking person standing behind you in line, and you say: _____

_____ ?

4. You are watching a videotape in class. Your classmate in front of you is in the way. You want

him or her to move his or her chair. You say: _____

_____ ?

5. Your teacher just showed the class a videotape. It is finished; your classroom is dark. Your

instructor wants the student who is sitting near the light switch to turn on the lights, so she or

he says: _____

_____ ?

6. There is a lot of noise outside your classroom. Your teacher wants the student who is sitting

near the door to close it, so she or he says: _____

_____ ?

7. A classmate is giving a presentation, but she is speaking very quietly. You cannot hear her. You

say: _____ ?

Focus 2

Making Polite Refusals

USE

- If you need to refuse a request, the refusal is more polite when: 1) you say **why** you have to refuse the request, and 2) you use a "softening" phrase.

Request	**"Softening" Phrase + Reason**
Can you lend me your notes?	**(a)** **I'm sorry**, but I need them to study for the test.
	(b) OR **I'm afraid** I didn't take any notes!
	(c) OR **I'd like to,** but I left mine at home too.

Exercise 2

Make requests of all your classmates and find someone who will grant your request (say yes) for the following things. For each request, try to find at least one person who will say yes. If a classmate says no, write down what the reason is for refusing your request (if a reason is given).

Request	Reason for Saying No
1. lend you some money	
2. buy you a cup of coffee	
3. tell you the name of a good bookstore	
4. give you a ride home after class	
5. teach you how to dance	

Focus 3

Responding to Requests

- To respond informally to requests, short answers are acceptable.

Request	Verbal Response
Can you lend me your notes?	**(a)** Sure.
	(b) You bet.
	(c) Yeah, no problem.
	(d) I'd be glad to.

- *Could* and *would* are usually not used in response to requests.

Can/Could you lend me your notes?	**(e)** Yes, I can NOT: Yes, I could.
Will/Would you lend me your notes?	**(f)** Yes, I will NOT: Yes, I would.

Exercise 3

Make polite requests for the following situations. Use *can, could, will, would,* or *would you mind* in these requests.

What is the response? How is the request politely accepted or refused?

1. You have a toothache. Your dentist asks you to sit back in the chair, open your mouth, and

   point to the tooth that hurts. The dentist says: _____

   _____ ?

   What do you do or say? _____

   _____ .

2. Your friend is helping you hang a picture on your wall. He is holding it up while you decide

where it should go. You say: _____

_____ ?

What does your friend do or say? _____

_____ .

3. At your first exercise class, the instructor asks you to use the wall to get your spine in a straight

position. The instructor says: _____

_____ ?

What do you do or say? _____

_____ .

4. There's a place on your back that suddenly begins to itch. You ask your close friend to scratch

it. You say: _____ ?

What does your friend do or say? _____

_____ .

But your friend is not quite getting the right place. So you say:_____

_____ ?

5. You are at a restaurant, and the people at the next table are smoking. You want them to stop, so

you say:_____

_____ ?

What do they do or say? _____

_____ .

Exercise 4

Place the following questions in the chart below, writing the number of each sentence in the appropriate box. The first one has been done for you.

Something the Speaker Wants to Do (request for permission)	Something the Speaker Wants Somebody Else to Do (general request)
1	

1. Could I smoke?
2. Can you open the window?
3. May I ask a question?
4. Could you speak more slowly?
5. Would you mind lending me your dictionary?
6. Can I leave early?
7. Would you tell me the answer?
8. May we swim in your pool?
9. Could you show us how to do it?
10. Could I borrow your knife?
11. Would you mind if I handed in my assignment a day late?

Focus 4

FORM ● USE

Asking for Permission

FORM
USE

- When you want **somebody** to do something, you can make a request. When **you** want to do something, and you want to find out if it is permitted or allowed, you can request permission:

  (a) Could I leave early?
  (b) Can I smoke in here?   } Is it all right if I do this?
  (c) May I ask a question?

- In formal situations, *may* or *could* are used in questions to request permission. If the speaker thinks that the listener has a lot of authority or power, she or he uses *may* or *could*.

- As with requests, *can* is used in informal situations to ask for permission. If the speaker and the listener know each other well and / or have an equal amount of power, *can* is used.

  You can also politely ask for permission using *Would you mind* + *if* + **simple past tense.**

  (d) Would you mind if I asked you a question?

Exercise 5

For each answer, what was probably the question?

1. Question: _____?

   Teacher to student: No, I'd like you to hand it in on Friday. I announced the due date two

   weeks ago, so I'm afraid I won't be able to make any exceptions.

2. Question: _____?

   Friend to friend: Sure, it is a little cold in here.

3. Question: _____?

   Lecturer to member of the audience: Sorry, but I'm going to have to ask you to hold your

   questions until the end of my talk. We'll have 15 minutes for questions.

4. Question: _____?

   Secretary (on phone): Yes, may I tell him who's calling?

5. Question: _____?

   12-year-old kid (on phone): Yeah, just a moment. I'll get him.

6. Question: _____?

   Mother (to child): OK, you can have one more. But only **one**, because we're going to eat soon
   and I don't want you to spoil your appetite.

7. Question: _____?

   Hostess to guest: Oh, of course, please help yourself. I'm glad you like them.

8. Question: _____?

   Customer to salesperson: Yes, I want to look at the sweaters that are on sale. The ones that were
   advertised in the newspaper?

Focus 5

FORM ● USE

Responding to Requests for Permission

FORM
USE

- As with responses to requests, you can verbally answer requests for permission with short, positive
  phrases:

  Sure.   OK.   Yeah.   Of course.   No problem.

- If you need to refuse a request for permission, the refusal is more polite when you say **why** you
  have to refuse the request, and you use a "softening" phrase such as *Sorry*.

Exercise 6

For each of the following situations, work with another classmate to make general requests and
requests for permission, and then respond to these requests. Decide how polite you need to be in
each situation and whether *can, could, will, would, may,* or *would you mind* is the most appropriate to
use. There is more than one way to ask and answer each question.

1. You are at a friend's house, and you want to use the phone.
2. Your teacher says something, but you do not understand, and you want her to repeat it.

174

3. Your friend has asked you to pick her up at the airport. You want to know if her flight, #255 from Denver, is on time, so you call the airline.

4. You want to borrow your roommate's car.

5. Your roommate is going to the store, and you remember that you need some film.

6. You are the first one to finish the reading test in class. You want to find out from your teacher if you are allowed to leave the room now.

7. It is very cold in class, and the window is open.

8. You see that your teacher is in her office with the door partly open. You want to go in to talk to her.

9. You are on the phone with the dentist's secretary because you want to change your appointment time.

10. You are at a close friend's house, and you would like a cup of tea.

11. Your friends have arrived at your house for dinner, and you want them to sit down.

12. You want to hold your friend's baby.

Activities

Activity 1

Go to a restaurant or cafeteria and pay attention to the different kinds of requests that are used. Try to observe five different requests. Take notes on these, using the chart below.

Observation Sheet		
Place: Time: Day:		
Request	**Who Made It**	**Response**

Discuss the results of your observations with other classmates. Were their observations similar? What words were used most often in requests: *can, could, will, would,* or *would you mind*?

Activity 2

Play this game in a group of five or six students or with the whole class. You are sick and cannot go out of your house. Choose a classmate and ask him or her to buy you something at the mall when she or he goes. Pick a letter from the alphabet. Your friend must think of something to buy that begins with the letter you choose, and then she or he must tell you what she or he will buy. She or he then chooses the next student and so on.

> EXAMPLE: **Shelley:** Bruno, would you please buy me something that begins with the letter *S*?
>
> **Bruno:** Sure. I'll buy you some stamps. Sue, could you buy me something that begins with the letter *M*?
>
> **Sue:** OK. I'll buy you a magazine. Hartmut, will you buy me something that begins with the letter *P*?

Activity 3

How do people request permission to speak with someone on the telephone? Are these ways different depending on the situation?

Make at least five observations to complete the following chart. If you cannot make direct observations, you can interview people about what they say in different situations.

Setting	Relationship	What They Say

Activity 4

Congratulations! You have just won a gift certificate for Easy-Does-It Maid Services. This entitles you to four hours of maid service for your home. First, make a list of what you want the maid to do in your home (clean your windows, do your laundry, scrub the toilet, etc.). Then, write these requests on a polite note to your "maid."

Appendix

<u>Irregular Verbs</u>

Simple Form	Past (-ed)	Past Participle	Simple Form	Past (-ed)	Past Participle
be	was, were	been	let	let	let
become	became	become	lie	lay	lain
begin	began	begun	light	lit, lighted	lit, lighted
bite	bit	bitten	lose	lost	lost
bleed	bled	bled	make	made	made
blow	blew	blown	meet	met	met
break	broke	broken	pay	paid	paid
bring	brought	brought	put	put	put
build	built	built	quit	quit	quit
buy	bought	bought	read	read	read
catch	caught	caught	ride	rode	ridden
choose	chose	chosen	ring	rang	rung
come	came	come	rise	rose	risen
cost	cost	cost	run	ran	run
cut	cut	cut	say	said	said
do	did	done	see	saw	seen
draw	drew	drawn	sell	sold	sold
drink	drank	drunk	send	sent	sent
drive	drove	driven	shine	shone	shone
eat	ate	eaten	show	showed	shown, showed
fall	fell	fallen	shut	shut	shut
feed	fed	fed	sing	sang	sung
feel	felt	felt	sit	sat	sat
fight	fought	fought	sleep	slept	slept
find	found	found	speak	spoke	spoken
fly	flew	flown	spend	spend	spent
forget	forgot	forgotten	stand	stood	stood
freeze	froze	frozen	steal	stole	stolen
get	got	got, gotten	swear	swore	sworn
give	gave	given	swim	swam	swum
go	went	gone	take	took	taken
grow	grew	grown	teach	taught	taught
have	had	had	tear	tore	torn
hear	heard	heard	tell	told	told
hide	hid	hidden	think	thought	thought
hit	hit	hit	throw	threw	thrown
hold	held	held	understand	understood	understood
hurt	hurt	hurt	upset	upset	upset
keep	kept	kept	wake	woke	woken, waked
know	knew	known	wear	worn	worn
lay	laid	laid	win	won	won
lead	led	led	write	wrote	written
leave	left	left			

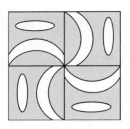

Index